Thr

Bible

BOOK BY BOOK

PART

OLD TESTAMENT

GENESIS TO ESTHER

ONE

Myer Pearlman

MY HEALTHY CHURCH

02-7001

© 2012 by My Healthy Church. All rights reserved.

Originally published © 1935 by Gospel Publishing House.

International Standard Book Number: 978-1-62423-000-4

Printed in the United States of America

FOREWORD

Through the Bible Book by Book, a classic introductory guide to understanding the 66 books of the Bible, has been translated into numerous languages. It has been a standard classroom text for more than seven decades in churches and schools, as well as an aid for personal Bible study.

The author, Myer Pearlman (1898-1943), was one of the foremost theologians in the Assemblies of God in the 1930s and 1940s. Raised in an observant Jewish family in Birmingham, England, he learned the Torah (Old Testament) and Hebrew as a boy. Pearlman's family moved to the United States when he was a teenager. After serving in the U.S. Army during World War I, Pearlman returned to America and accepted Christ at a small Pentecostal mission in San Francisco.

Pearlman enrolled at the newly opened Central Bible Institute (now Central Bible College, Springfield, Missouri) in 1922. Upon graduation, the principal, Frank M. Boyd, invited Pearlman to join the faculty.

Noted for his prolific pen, Pearlman authored numerous textbooks and the early years of the Assemblies of God adult Sunday school curriculum. At a time when anti-Semitism was on the rise in Europe and in America, it is significant that the Assemblies of God entrusted a Jewish-born theologian with such a significant responsibility. Pearlman's background, however, made him a uniquely qualified biblical scholar within the Pentecostal movement.

After years of constant writing, teaching and preaching, Pearlman literally worked himself to death. Myer Pearlman died on July 16, 1943, in Springfield, Missouri.

Darrin J. Rodgers, Director
Flower Pentecostal Heritage Center

ABBREVIATIONS FOR
THE BOOKS OF THE BIBLE

Old Testament

Genesis	Gen.
Exodus	Ex.
Leviticus	Lev.
Numbers	Num.
Deuteronomy	Deut.
Joshua	Josh.
Judges	Jud.
Ruth	Ruth
1 Samuel	1 Sam.
2 Samuel	2 Sam.
1 Kings	1 Kings
2 Kings	2 Kings
1 Chronicles	1 Chron.
2 Chronicles	2 Chron.
Ezra	Ezra
Nehemiah	Neh.
Esther	Est.
Job	Job
Psalms	Ps.
Proverbs	Prov.
Ecclesiastes	Ecc.
Song of Solomon	S. of Sol.
Isaiah	Isa.
Jeremiah	Jer.
Lamentations	Lam.
Ezekiel	Ezek.
Daniel	Dan.
Hosea	Hosea
Joel	Joel
Amos	Amos
Obadiah	Oba.
Jonah	Jonah
Micah	Micah

Nahum	Nahum
Habbakuk	Hab.
Zephaniah	Zeph.
Haggai	Hag.
Zechariah	Zech.
Malachi	Mal.

New Testament

Matthew	Matt.
Mark	Mark
Luke	Luke
John	John
Acts of the Apostles	Acts
Romans	Rom.
1 Corinthians	1 Cor.
2 Corinthians	2 Cor.
Galatians	Gal.
Ephesians	Eph.
Philippians	Phil.
Colossians	Col.
1 Thessalonians	1 Thess.
2 Thessalonians	2 Thess.
1 Timothy	1 Tim.
2 Timothy	2 Tim.
Titus	Titus
Philemon	Phile.
Hebrews	Heb.
James	James
1 Peter	1 Peter
2 Peter	2 Peter
1 John	1 John
2 John	2 John
3 John	3 John
Jude	Jude
Revelation	Rev.

CHAPTER I

Learn the books of the Old Testament.

1. The Pentateuch
- (1) Genesis
- (2) Exodus
- (3) Leviticus
- (4) Numbers
- (5) Deuteronomy

2. The Historical Books
- (1) Joshua
- (2) Judges
- (3) Ruth
- (4) 1 Samuel
- (5) 2 Samuel
- (6) 1 Kings
- (7) 2 Kings
- (8) 1 Chronicles
- (9) 2 Chronicles
- (10) Ezra
- (11) Nehemiah
- (12) Esther

3. The Poetical Books
- (1) Job
- (2) Psalms
- (3) Proverb
- (4) Ecclesiastes
- (5) Song of Solomon

4. The Major Prophetical Books
- (1) Isaiah
- (2) Jeremiah
- (3) Lamentations
- (4) Ezekiel
- (5) Daniel

5. The Minor Prophetical Books
- (1) Hosea
- (2) Joel
- (3) Amos
- (4) Obadiah
- (5) Jonah
- (6) Micah
- (7) Nahum
- (8) Habakkuk
- (9) Zephaniah
- (10) Haggai
- (11) Zechariah
- (12) Malachi

GENESIS

Theme. The book is well described by its title, Genesis, which means "beginning," for it is a history of the beginning of all things—the beginning of heaven and earth, of all life and of all human institutions and relations. It has been called the seed-plot of the Bible from the fact that the germs of all the great doctrines concerning God, man, sin and salvation are found there.

The very first verse suggests the purpose of the book. "In the beginning God created the heaven and the earth." The Israelites, to whom the message of the book was first addressed, would learn that the God of **Palestine** was also the God of **all lands**, and that the God of **one nation**—Israel—was also the God of **all nations**. Since He was the God and Creator of all the earth, He must ultimately become the Redeemer of all the earth. The book describes how redemption became necessary because man had sinned and fallen into darkness; and how God prepared to choose one nation to take the light of Divine truth to the other nations.

Author. Moses

Scope. From the Creation to the death of Joseph, covering a period of 2,315 years, from about 4004 BC to 1689 BC.

CONTENTS

The contents of Genesis center around nine outstanding subjects.

    I.   The Creation (Chaps. 1, 2)
    II.   The Fall (Chap. 3)
    III. The First Civilization (Chap. 4)
    IV. The Flood (Chaps. 5–9)
    V.   The Dispersion of Nations (Chaps. 10, 11)
    VI. Abraham (Chaps. 12–25)
    VII. Isaac (Chaps. 17–35)
   VIII. Jacob (Chaps. 25–35)
    IX. Joseph (Chaps. 27–50)

We shall now analyze the chapters covering each point of the above outline and in so doing we shall be able to fix in our minds the most important facts.

I. The Creation (Chaps. 1, 2)

The great Architect of the universe completed His work of creation in six days, and rested on the seventh. The following is the order of the creation:

Preparation and Separation		Completion and Filling	
1st Day	Light	4th Day	Lights (heavenly bodies)
2nd Day	Air	5th Day	Birds
	Water		Fish
3rd Day	Land	6th Day	Animals
	Plants		Man

On the seventh day He ceased, setting man an example of laboring six days and resting on the seventh.

After creating man, the crown of creation, God pronounced everything **very** good. Chapter two tells how God prepared man's first home, performed the first wedding ceremony and placed two trees in the garden, that taught the following lessons: if Adam and his wife chose the **good** and refused the EVIL, they would always eat of the tree of **life**; otherwise, they would die.

In chapter 2, we find a repetition of the account of creation. On comparing the two chapters, however, we shall see that chapter 1 gives us a general account of the event, while chapter 2 gives the same account with the addition of extra details and with the emphasizing of some particular part of the story. This peculiarity of the Holy Spirit in giving two accounts of one event is called the "Law of recurrence" and is found all through the Bible.

What does chapter 2 tell concerning the creation that chapter 1 omits? What is meant by man being created in the image of God? (See Eph. 4:24; Col. 3:10). To whom does "us" refer in the expression, "Let us make man"? (Read Job 35:10; Col. 1:16; Job 33:4).

II. The Fall (Chap. 3)

Notice—

1. The possibility of temptation. The tree of the knowledge of **good** and **evil** was left in the garden in order that man might be tested and learn to serve God from a willing heart.

2. The author of the temptation. The serpent represents, and is an agent of, "that great serpent the devil."

3. The subtlety of the temptation. The serpent succeeded in injecting a question mark in the mind of Eve.

4. The success of the temptation. Adam and Eve disobeyed God and became conscious of guilt.

5. The first judgment.

a. On the serpent: degradation.

b. On the woman: pain, and subjection to man.

c. On the man: hard labor on a thorn-bearing ground until his death.

d. On man and his descendants: exclusion from the tree of life in the paradise of God.

6. The first announcement of redemption.

a. Redemption promised: Gen. 3:15. "I will put enmity between thee and the woman, and between thy seed and her seed." That is, there will be a struggle between mankind and the power that caused his fall. "It shall bruise thy head"—mankind will be victorious, through its representative, the Son of Man. See Acts 10:38; 1 John 3:8. "And thou shalt bruise his heel"—but the victory will be through suffering, through the death of the Seed of the woman, Christ. See also Gal. 4:4; Isa. 7:14; Matt. 1:21.

b. Redemption pictured. The Lord slew the first sacrifice in order to clothe the guilty pair—a picture of the covering of a guilty conscience through blood sacrifice.

Note: the book of Genesis is the record of the development of this promise of redemption, showing how it passed through different individuals and families.

III. The First Civilization (Chap. 4)

1. **The story of Cain** shows how sin became hereditary, and led to the first murder. See 1 John 3:12.

2. **The story of Abel** teaches us how those sharing in Adam's guilt and sinfulness may be accepted in God's sight—through the offering of an atoning sacrifice.

3. **The first civilization.** Cain became the founder of a civilization that included a city, agriculture, manufacturing, and arts. In character it was marked by violation of the marriage law and by the spirit of violence. 4:19–24.

4. **The birth of Seth.** Abel was dead; Cain was rejected; the promise of redemption passed on to Adam's third son, Seth. 4:25, 26.

IV. The Flood (Chaps. 5-9)

There were now two classes of people in the world—the ungodly Cainites and the godly Sethites. See 4:25, 26. The chosen line of Seth lost its separation and intermarried with the Cainites. Result: a condition of wickedness on the earth that called for God's judgment. Of Seth's descendants only the family of Noah remained true to God. Noah becomes the chosen one through whom the promise of redemption continued its journey toward fulfillment (5:29; 6:8).

Note the genealogy in chapter 5. (Genealogy is the record of descent from some ancestor.) It begins with Adam and ends with Noah. We shall find many of these genealogies in the Bible. The main purpose of most of them, as of the one in this chapter, is to keep a record of the line through which the promised Seed (Christ) was to come (Gen. 3:15).

Let us sum up the main events of these chapters. Learn these:

1. The genealogy of Noah (Chap. 5)
2. The building of the ark (Chap. 6)
3. The entrance into the ark (Chap. 7)
4. The departure from the ark (Chap. 8)
5. The covenant with Noah (Chap. 9)

Notice the high state of civilization at the time of the Flood (Chap. 4:16–24). The descendants of Cain were the builders of the first city and the originators of the first arts. What are those days to remind us of? (See Matt. 24:37–39).

God destroyed the world with a flood, and started a new race with the family of Noah. He promised that the earth should never again be destroyed by a flood, and made the rainbow the seal of that covenant. The Lord renewed the charge made to Adam; namely, to replenish the earth. There is a solemn prohibition of murder with this addition that "whoso sheddeth man's blood, by man shall his blood be shed." This marks the delegating of authority to man to govern his fellows and visit punishment upon crime. Before this, it was God alone who punished evildoers.

Later Noah predicted the future of his three sons (9:18–27) and appointed Shem as the chosen seed through whom God would bless the world.

V. The Dispersion of the Nations (Chaps. 10, 11)

As an introduction of the study of the nations,

read again carefully Noah's prophecy concerning his three sons (Chap. 9:24–27).

Dr. Pinnock writes of its fulfillment as follows:

These prophecies have been wonderfully fulfilled. In respect of **Ham's** posterity: the Egyptians were afflicted with various plagues; the land of **Canaan** eight hundred years afterwards was delivered by God into the hands of the Israelites under Joshua, who destroyed great numbers, and obliged the rest to flee, some into Africa, and others into various countries; their present condition in Africa we now know.

In respect of **Japheth:** 'God shall enlarge Japheth,' has been fulfilled in the vast extent of country possessed by him—all the isles and countries westward; and when the Greeks, and afterwards the Romans, subdued Asia and Africa, they then occupied the dwellings of Shem and of Canaan.

In respect of **Shem:** 'Blessed be the Lord God of Shem'—that is, He and His church should dwell in the tents of Shem; from him should spring the Messiah; and the worship of the true God should be preserved among his posterity; the Jews being the posterity of Shem.

Notice the relation of chapter 10 to chapter 11. Chapter 10 indicates the separate locations of the races and chapter 11 explains how the separation occurred.

After the Flood, the descendants of Noah, led by Nimrod (10:8–10), rose in rebellion against God, as an outward sign of which they erected the Tower of Babel. Their purpose was to organize a "league of nations" against God. God spoiled their plan by confounding their speech and scattering them in different countries.

We may speculate in vain as to the exact purpose of the tower itself, but this we may know, that their project was an act of rebellion against God. It was evidently God's purpose that the descendants of

Noah should spread abroad and occupy the different countries of the earth. (See Acts 17:26 and Deut. 32:8). But they said, "Let us make us a name, lest we be scattered abroad." Who was the probable instigator of this rebellion? (See ch. 10:8, 9.) What was his kingdom? (Chap. 10:10). Of whom is he a type? (2 Thess 2:3–11; Rev. 13). Who, in rebellion, will gather the nations together in the last days? (Rev. 16:13–15). Will Babel (or Babylon) again be prominent in the last days? (See Rev. 17, 18).

Learn the following simple outline of chapters 10 and 11:

1. The unity of race and speech.
2. The location of the event—the land of Shinar.
3. The purpose of the tower of Babel—to be a center of rebellion against God.
4. God's judgment—the confusion of tongues.
5. The result of the judgment—dispersion.

VI. Abraham (Chaps. 12-25)

It will be interesting to observe that the first eleven chapters of Genesis cover about 2,000 years—about equal in length to that time covered by all the rest of the Bible. Why does the Spirit hurry so over the events of the dawn of history? Because, as we found out in our earlier in this chapter, the Bible is mainly a history of redemption, and the history of nations is only incidental to that subject. The Spirit hurries over all these events till He comes to Abraham. Then He stops and devotes more space to that one person than He does to 2,000 years of human history. The reason is obvious. The "Father of the Faithful" plays an important role in the history of redemption.

By way of review turn back to Genesis Chap. 5. We called attention there to the genealogy of Noah beginning with Adam. Now turn to 11:10–26, and you will find that this list is continued. God is still keeping a record of the ancestors of the "Seed of the woman." With the name of what one important person does this list end (v. 26)? Why? (see Gen. 12:2, 3).

The promise of Gen. 3:15 passed on to Abraham. God separated him from his heathen surroundings, and besides personal promises, made the following national and universal promises (See 12:1–3):

    a. That he should be given a land (Canaan).

    b. That he should be the father of a nation (Israel).

    c. That through this nation in this land all nations of the earth should be blessed. In other words, the Redeemer promised in 3:15 should come from a nation descended from Abraham.

A study of the life of Abraham will reveal that it is a life of faith—a faith that was tested from the time that he was called to the time when he was commanded to sacrifice his son, Isaac. His life is an illustration of the type of person who would receive the blessing promised in 12:3, and a prophecy of the truth that salvation should be through faith. See Galatians 3:8; Romans Chap. 4.

In this study we shall have time to give only the bare outline of the life of this patriarch. Since you have read the chapters, the details will suggest themselves. Learn the following facts:

    1. His call to go to Canaan (Gen. 12:1–5)

    2. His descent into Egypt and happenings while there (12:10–20)

    3. His separation from Lot and his subsequent deliverance of the latter from captivity (13:5–11; 14:14)

    4. His reception of God's covenant and his justification by faith (15:6, 18)

5. His circumcision as a sign of the covenant (17:9–14)
6. The annunciation of Isaac's birth. (17:15–19; 18:1–15)
7. His intercession for Sodom (18:23–33)
8. His dismissal of Hagar and Ishmael (21:14)
9. His offering up of Isaac (22)
10. His choice of a bride for Isaac (24)
11. His children by Keturah (Chap. 25:1–4)
12. His death (Chap. 25:8)

VII. Isaac (Chaps. 17–35)

To Abraham were born two sons—Ishmael and Isaac. Of these, Isaac was chosen as the inheritor of the promise.

The life of Isaac is quiet and uneventful, and it seems to be a mere echo of his father's. Yet, like his father he is a man of faith, and a channel of blessing. Notice that the promise is repeated to him (Chap. 26).

Learn the following six facts concerning Isaac:

1. His birth promised to Abraham and Sarah (Chap. 15:4; 17:19)
2. Bound upon an altar of sacrifice (Chap. 22:9)
3. Abraham's choice of a bride for him (Chap. 24)
4. God appears to him and renews the covenant made to his father (Chap. 26:2–5)
5. His deception by Jacob (Chap. 27:18)
6. His death (Chap. 35:28, 29)

What was Isaac's birth a type of (Gen. 18:9–15 and Matt. 1:21)? His going to Mt. Moriah to be sacrificed (Compare Gen. 22 and Matt. 27:22, 23)? His deliverance from death (Gen. 22; Matt. 28:1–6)? His father's sending his servant to seek a bride for him (Gen. 24; Acts 15:14; 1 Cor. 12:13; Eph. 5:25, 26, 32).

VIII. Jacob (Chaps. 25–35)

To Isaac were born two sons—Esau and Jacob, Esau was rejected, and Jacob was chosen as the channel of blessing (25:23). The character of these two sons is revealed by their attitude toward this promise. See 25:29–34.

Learn the outstanding events of Jacob's life:
1. His purchase of his brother's birthright (25:33)
2. His deception of his father (27:18–27)
3. His flight to Padan-aram (27:43 to 28:5)
4. His vision and vow (28:10)
5. His dealings with Laban (Chap. 31)
6. His wrestling with an angel (32:24)
7. His reconcilation with Esau (Chap. 33)
8. His descent into Egypt and his meeting with Joseph (Chap. 46)
9. His death and burial (49:33 to 50:13)

Jacob is the true father of the chosen people, for to him were born the twelve sons that became the fathers of the twelve tribes. And notice that he is a remarkable type of the nation in its character and experiences:

a. Notice the combination of shrewd business ability and the desire for the knowledge of God. Consider how these two characteristics are revealed in Jacob's attempts to gain possession of the birthright and blessing. And remember that the Jews have been **the** religious nation, and also **the** business nation.

b. Jacob was an exile from his own land for about twenty years. The Jews as a whole have been exiled from their land about nineteen hundred years.

c. Jacob went into exile with a promise that the Lord would bring him back, in order to fulfill the promise made to Abraham. So Israel's restoration has been assured. They are beloved for the sake of Abraham, Isaac and Jacob (Rom. 11:28).

d. God's plan was fulfilled through Jacob in spite of the defects of his character. So shall it be with Israel as a nation. As Jacob's character was transformed, so will that of his descendants.

Some important lessons may be learned from the life of Jacob.

1. The power of the grace of God. Jacob was all that his name meant—a supplanter, a deceiver. The sacred ties of family were no bar to his scheming, for his father and his brother fell victims to his deceit. But through the dross of Jacob's sinfulness, God saw the glint of that which has been likened to fine gold—faith. At the brook Jabbok, the Grace of God engaged in battle with him, and in the struggle which ensued, the sinful Jacob died, but from his grave rose a new creature—Israel, an overcomer with God and man.

2. God's high estimate of faith. Though the scheming of Jacob to obtain his brother's birthright is inexcusable, yet his earnest desire for it showed an appreciation of spiritual things. To him, the birthright carried with it the honor of being the progenitor of the Messiah, and his longing for that honor we may well regard as an expression of faith in the Coming One. It was this faith that gave him preference before God over his brother, Esau, who, though in many respects a more noble man than he, showed an utter lack of appreciation of spiritual values by selling for a mess of pottage the right of becoming the progenitor of the "Desire of all nations."

3. "Whatsoever a man soweth, that shall he also reap." Jacob's uncle, Laban, was in the hands of God an instrument of retribution for the disciplining of Jacob. Jacob had cheated others; he, in turn, was cheated. He found in his uncle a mirror that reflected back upon him his own deceitfulness.

IX. Joseph (Chaps. 30-50)

The story of Joseph, a boy of seventeen, favored by his father, Israel, who outwardly manifested his affection and esteem, and so caused jealousy on the part of the other sons. Joseph was also favored by the Lord, who revealed to him through dreams that he would be ruler over the other members of his family. This enraged his brothers, who sold him into Egypt, where after much adversity and temptation, and years of waiting for the fulfillment of the promise, he was exalted as the second ruler of the land of Egypt. When his brothers came down for grain and bowed before him, his dreams were fulfilled.

The meaning of the story. Joseph's experiences were connected with the plan of redemption that we have already mentioned. God permitted him to be sold into Egypt and to suffer, in order that he might be exalted and thus have an opportunity to nourish the chosen family during famine and settle them in a territory where they could grow into a great nation and undergo certain experiences, until Jehovah was ready to lead them to the conquest of the Promised Land. See Genesis 45:7, 8; 50:20.

Learn the following brief outline of the life of Joseph:

1. Loved by his father (37:3)
2. Envied by his brethren (37:4)
3. Sold to the Ishmaelites (37:18-36)
4. Favored by his master (39:1-6)
5. Tempted by his master's wife (39:7-19)
6. Imprisoned by Potiphar (39:20 to 41:13)
7. Exalted by Pharaoh (41:1-44)
8. Unrecognized by brethren at first meeting (42:7 to 44:34)
9. Revealed to brethren at second meeting (45:1-15)

   10. Reunited to his father, Jacob (46:28–34)

   11. His death (50:22–26)

The life of Joseph presents some striking types of Christ. Of what is his father's love for him a type (Gen. 37:3; John 5:20)? The hatred of his brethren (Matt. 27:1, 22, 23)? His temptation (Matt. 4:1)? His patience in suffering (James 5:10, 11)? His promotion by Pharaoh (Mark 16:19)? His marrying a Gentile bride during his rejection by his brethren (Acts 15:14)? His revelation of himself to his brethren the second time (Zech. 12:10)?

CHAPTER II

EXODUS

Title. Exodus comes from Greek words meaning "going out," and was so named because it recorded the departure of Israel from Egypt.

Theme. In the book of Genesis we read about the **beginnings** of redemption. In the book of Exodus we read about the **progress** of redemption. In Genesis this redemption is being worked out through **individuals;** in Exodus, it is worked out through an entire nation—Israel. The central thought of the book is redemption by blood. Around this thought gathers the story of a people saved by the Blood, sheltered by the Blood and having access unto God by the Blood. This redemption is shown to meet every need of the nation. Oppressed by the Egyptians, Israel needs deliverance. God supplies this deliverance. Having been saved, the nation needs a revelation from God to guide them in conduct and worship in their new life. God gives them the Law. Convicted of sin by the holiness of the Law, the Israelites find their need of cleansing. God provides sacrifices. Having a revelation of God, the people feel their need of worship. God gives them the tabernacle and appoints a priesthood.

Author. Moses

Scope. The events recorded in Exodus cover a period of 216 years, from about 1706 BC to 1490 BC. It begins with an enslaved people dwelling in the presence of Egyptian idolatry, and ends with a redeemed people dwelling in the presence of God.

CONTENTS

We shall now try to obtain a bird's-eye view of the book of Exodus in order to see the book as a whole. Learn the following outline:

    I.   Israel in Bondage (Chaps. 1, 2)
   II.   Israel Redeemed (Chaps. 3 to 15:22)
  III.   Israel Journeying to Sinai (Chaps. 15:23 to 19)
  IV.   Israel Given the Law (Chaps. 20–23)
   V.   Israel in Worship (Chaps. 24–40)

Let us now analyze each point of our outline.

I. Israel in Bondage (Chaps. 1, 2)

The following is a summary of chapters 1 and 2:
1. The oppression of Israel (Chap. 1)
2. The birth of Moses (2:1–4)
3. The adoption of Moses (2:5–10)
4. The ill-advised zeal of Moses (2:11–14)
5. The flight of Moses (2:15)
6. The marriage of Moses (2:16–22)

Was Israel's bondage prophesied (Gen. 15:7–16)? What did this bondage do for Israel (Ex. 2:23)? What would this result in (Rom. 10:13)? Did Moses ever forget his people and his God while being educated in Egypt (Heb. 11:24–26)? Why not (Ex. 2:7–9)? What did he suppose when he killed the Egyptian (Acts 7:25)? Was it God's time? What did Moses' forty years' sojourn in the wilderness teach him? (Compare Acts 7:25 and Ex. 3:11).

II. Israel Redeemed (Chaps. 3 to 15)

1. The call and commission of Moses (3 to 4:28)
2. His departure to Egypt (4:24–31)
3. His conflict with Pharaoh (Chaps. 5 and 6)
4. The plagues (Chaps. 7 to 11)

5. The Passover (Chap. 12)
6. The departure from Egypt (Chap. 13)
7. The crossing of the Red Sea (14 to 15:21)

Notice the greatness and the supernatural character of Israel's deliverance. God's purpose was to have a people whose testimony to the world would be, "Saved by the power of God." He wanted so to impress the event upon the mind of Israel that in the days to come, when the oppression and trial should come, they could always look and remember that "salvation is of the Lord." In the Old Testament, God's deliverance of Israel from Egypt is the measure of His power. What is the measure of His power in the New Testament (Eph. 1:19, 20; Phil. 3:10)?

The explanation of a difficulty is in order here. Many have stumbled at the fact that God hardened Pharaoh's heart and then punished him. Let it be noted that Pharaoh hardened his own heart also (Chap. 8:15, 32). God hardened Pharaoh's heart in the same sense that the Gospel hardens men's hearts when they reject it. To some, the Gospel brings salvation, to others death. (See 2 Cor. 2:15, 16). In Acts 19:9 we read that "divers were hardened" after Paul had preached. Could Paul be blamed for the hardness of their hearts? No, the blame rests with those who rejected the message. So it was in the case of Pharaoh. God's message was simply the **occasion** of the hardening of his heart; his own refusal to obey the message was the **cause**.

The Passover contains some wonderful types of our redemption. What does Egypt typify (Gal. 1:4; Rom. 6:18)? The lamb (John 1:29)? The blood sprinkled on the door posts (Rom. 3:25; 1 Peter 1:18–20)? The unleavened bread (1 Cor. 5:8)? The eating of the lamb (1 Cor. 11:24)? The crossing of the Red Sea (1 Cor. 10:1, 2)?

III. Israel Journeying to Sinai (Chaps. 15–18)

In this study it will be well to consult a map of the journey.

Summary of Chapters 15 to 18:

1. Marah—Bitter waters (Chap. 15)
2. Elim—Wells and trees (Chap. 15)
3. Wilderness of Sin—Manna (Chap. 16)
4. Rephidim—Rock smitten; battle with Amalek (Chap. 17)
5. Sinai—Visit of Jethro (Chap. 18)

IV. Israel Given the Law (Chaps. 19–23)

Summary of Chapters 19–23:

1. Moses ascent to Sinai (Chap. 19)
2. The Ten Commandments (Chap. 20)
3. The civil law (Chaps. 21–23)

Study the following topics:

I. Israel's election. Ex. 19:5. By a solemn covenant Israel was appointed the priest-nation—separated **from** all nations, in order to be trained in Divine truth and ultimately bring light **to** all nations.

II. Israel's legislation. Ex. 20–23. Just as the United States of America is a republic governed on the basis of its Constitution, so Israel was a theocracy (a state governed by God) having as the basis of its government the Ten Commandments, which we may regard as the Constitution of the United Tribes of Israel. The commandments represent the tenfold expression of the will of Jehovah, and the standard by which He rules His subjects. In order to apply these principles to the everyday life of the people, the civil law was added, which prescribed penalties and gave directions for enforcement.

What did the Israelites undertake to do (Ex. 19:8)? Could they do this (Acts 13:38; Gal. 2:16)? Why not (Rom. 7:14; 8:3)? If they could not keep the Law, why was it given (Rom. 3:19, 20; 5:20; Gal. 3:24)? What two principal lessons was the Law intended to teach (Matt. 22:37–39)? Then how do Christians fulfill the Law (Rom. 13:8–10)? How may we possess the love that fulfills it (Rom. 5:5; Gal. 5:18)? Under what Law is the Christian (Gal. 6:2; John 15:12)?

V. Israel in Worship (Chaps. 24-40)

1. Moses receives pattern for tabernacle (Chaps. 24–31)
2. The law broken (Chaps. 32–34)
3. The tabernacle under construction (Chaps. 35–39)
4. The tabernacle erected (Chap. 40)

At Mount Sinai Jehovah and His people entered into a special relationship. Through the mediatorship of Moses, a redeemed people and their God were united in the holy bonds of covenant relationship. Jehovah became the God of Israel, and Israel became the people of Jehovah. In order that fellowship might be continued, Jehovah commanded the erection of the tabernacle. "And let them make Me a sanctuary; that I may dwell among them." Ex. 25:8. The design of the tabernacle will be more clearly understood as we consider the titles applied to it:

a. The Tabernacle (in Hebrew, "dwelling"). Though God dwells everywhere, He appointed a place where His people could always find Him "at home."

b. The Tent of the Congregation or the Tent of Meeting. It was the point of contact and the channel of communication between heaven and earth (Ex. 29:42, 43).

c. The Tabernacle of Testimony, or the Tent of Witness. It was so called from the presence of the two tables of the Law which were placed in the ark. These tables were called the "testimony" (Ex. 31:18; 34:29). They witnessed to God's holiness and man's sinfulness.

d. The Sanctuary. Literally, "holy place," or a building set apart for the Divine indwelling.

CHAPTER III
LEVITICUS

Title. The book of Leviticus is so called because it is a record of laws pertaining to the Levites and their service.

Theme. In Exodus we saw Israel redeemed; redemption of an enslaved people. Leviticus tells us how a redeemed people can approach God in worship and how the fellowship thus established can be maintained. The message of Leviticus is access to God is only through blood, and access thus obtained calls for holiness on the part of the worshiper. Most of the types in the book relate to the atoning work of Christ, and are set forth in the various offerings there described. Exodus gives us the account of one offering that pointed to Christ our Passover. Leviticus gives us many offerings pointing us to the different aspects of redemption. The message of the book is well stated in Lev. 19:2. Note the practical purpose of the book: it contains a divinely appointed code of laws designed to make Israel different from other nations, spiritually, morally, mentally and physically. In other words Israel was to become a holy nation—a nation separated from the ways and customs of the nations surrounding them and consecrated to the service of the one true God.

Author. Moses

Scope. The book embraces the period of less than a year of Israel's sojourn at Sinai.

CONTENTS

Leviticus is a book of laws, so we may classify its contents with that thought in mind.

I.   Laws Concerning Offerings (Chaps. 1–7)
II. Laws Concerning Priesthood (Chaps. 8–10)
III. Laws Concerning Purification (Chaps. 11–22)
IV. Laws Concerning Feasts (Chaps. 23, 24)
V.   Laws Concerning the Land (Chaps. 25–27)

I.   Laws Concerning the Offerings (Chaps. 1-7)

Sacrifices were instituted as means whereby the people could express their worship of God:

1. The burnt offering signified entire consecration to Jehovah.
2. The peace offering, part of which was eaten by the priest and part by the offerer, pictured fellowship with his God.
3. The meat [grain] offering, or food offering, consisting of flour, cakes or grain, represented the offering of a gift to the Lord of all in acknowledgment of His goodness.
4. By means of the sin offering the Israelite expressed sorrow for sin and the desire for pardon and cleansing.
5. The trespass offering was brought in the case of offences that called for restitution.

II. Laws Concerning the Priesthood (Chaps. 8-10)

These chapters record the consecration of Aaron and his sons and their inauguration into the priestly office. The following are the main topics of this section:

1. Consecration (Chap. 8). The consecration ceremonies included washing with water, clothing with priestly garments, anointing with oil, the offering of sacrifices, and the sprinkling of blood.
2. The service (Chap. 9)
3. The failure (Chap. 10). Nadab and Abihu, Aaron's sons, instead of using fire taken from the altar, used ordinary fire for the burning

of the incense. In order to impress the nation with the sacredness and responsibility of the priesthood, God made an example of these men by destroying them with fire. What probably led to their sin? See verses 8–11. Does 1 Corinthians 11:20–32 suggest some parallels?

III. Laws Concerning Purity (Chaps. 11–22)

Let us sum up this section as follows. Israel as a holy nation have—

1. Holy food (Chap. 11)
2. Holy bodies (12:1 to 14:32)
3. Holy homes (14:33–57)
4. Holy habits (Chap. 15)
5. Holiness annually renewed (Chap. 16)
6. Holy worship (17:1–16)
7. Holy morals (Chap. 18)
8. Holy customs and costumes (Chaps. 19–22)

What does chapter 18 teach concerning the character of the nations surrounding Israel? (See verses 24, 28). Many infidels have taken exception to the contents of these chapters, characterizing them as improper. But let it be noted that the Bible, in describing moral diseases, does not resort to prudery or mock-modesty any more than does a medical text-book in dealing with physical diseases.

IV. Laws Concerning Feasts (Chaps. 23, 24)

1. The Sabbath (23:1–3). We may consider this day as the weekly feast of the Israelites, on which they rested from all work, and on which they gathered for worship.

2. The Passover and the feast of unleavened bread. Notice that there were two feasts in one—the Passover (celebrating the passing of the death-angel over the houses of the Israelites), which lasted one day; and the Feast of Unleavened Bread (commemorating the departure from Egypt), which lasted seven days.

3. Following close after the last named feast came the firstfruits, when a sheaf of the firstfruits of the harvest was waved before the Lord. This was a type of the resurrection of Christ (1 Cor. 15:20).

4. Fifty days after the firstfruits came the feast of Pentecost (meaning "fifty"). On the fiftieth day, two wave loaves, with leaven (23:17) were offered before the Lord.

5. The Feast of Trumpets (23:23–25), "New Year's Day." Look up the following references and find out the typical signification of this feast (Isa. 27:13; 1 Cor. 15:52; Matt. 24:31; Rev. 11:15)

6. The Day of Atonement (Lev. 23:27–32). (Read also Leviticus 16 and Hebrews 9:6–12). This was rather a fast than a feast. On that day the high priest entered the Holy of Holies, with blood, to make expiation for the sins of the people. This was done but once a year, and it typified Christ's entering heaven itself with His own blood to make eternal atonement for our sins. Besides the other sacrifices of that day, there were two goats. One of these was killed; upon the other, Aaron laid his hands, confessing over it the sins of the nation, and then sent it into the wilderness. These two goats represented two aspects of the atonement. The first typified Christ as paying the penalty for our sins—death; the second, as putting away our sins, never to remember them again.

7. The Feast of Tabernacles (Lev. 23:33–44) commemorated the days when the Israelites lived in tents, after their departure from Egypt. As this feast followed the harvest (23:39), we may take it to typify the rejoicing of the saints in the presence of the Lord, after the great gathering. (Compare the references to palms in verse 40 and Rev. 7:9).

Note the typical sequence of the feasts—how they give the history of redemption. We shall omit the Day of Atonement, for it is not a feast, but a fast.

> Passover—The crucifixion
> Firstfruits—The resurrection of Christ
> Pentecost—The outpouring of the Spirit
> Trumpets—The rapture of the living, and resurrection of the dead, saints
> Tabernacles—Our dwelling in the presence of the Lord after the great gathering

V. Laws Concerning the Land (Chaps. 25-27)

1. The year of the Jubilee (Chap. 25)
2. Reward and punishment (Chap. 26)
3. Vows (Chap. 27)

The year of Jubilee was a sabbatical year held every fifty years and beginning on the Day of Atonement. At that time, the land was given rest from cultivation, all debts were canceled, all Hebrew slaves were released, all estates reverted to their original owners. Houses in walled towns were an exception; they did not revert (25:30). The purpose of the Jubilee was to prevent the perpetual enslavement of the poor, and the accumulation of wealth by the rich; and likewise to preserve the distinction of the tribes and their tribal possessions. It was that year which Christ proclaimed as "the acceptable year of the Lord" (Luke 4:19) and by Peter as "the times of the restitution of all things" (Acts 3:21). As a type, the Jubilee finds its partial fulfillment in this Gospel dispensation, and its complete fulfillment during the Millennium.

In Chapter 26, on what is Israel's blessing conditioned (v. 3)? When were vv. 28–39 completely fulfilled (Luke 21:20–24)? When will Jehovah turn to Israel again (v. 40)? When will that take place (Zech. 12:10; Rev. 1:7)? Even though scattered and under punishment, is Israel forsaken of Jehovah (vv. 44, 45)? What will He remember (42)?

CHAPTER IV

NUMBERS

Title. The book of Numbers is so called because it contains the record of the two numberings of Israel before entering Canaan.

Theme. In Exodus we saw Israel redeemed; in Leviticus, Israel worshiping; and now in Numbers we see Israel serving. The service of the Lord was not to be done in any haphazard manner, so the book gives us a spectacle of a camp where everything is done according to the first law of heaven—order. The people are numbered, according to tribes and families; every tribe is assigned its position in camp; the marching and encampment of the people are regulated with military precision; and in the transporting of the tabernacle, every Levite had his appointed task. Besides being a book of service and order, Numbers is a book recording Israel's failure to believe God's promises and enter Canaan, and of their wandering in the wilderness as a punishment. But it is a failure that does not thwart God's plans, for the end of the book leaves us at the borders of the Promised Land, where the new generation of Israelites awaits to enter. Thus four words—service, order, failure, wandering—will sum up the message of Numbers.

Author. Moses

Scope. Thirty-nine years of Israel's wandering in the wilderness from about 1490 to 1451 BC.

CONTENTS

We shall outline Numbers according to the principal journeys of Israel. In these studies it is suggested that the student use a map in locating the different places mentioned in the course of his reading.

   I.   At Sinai (Chaps. 1–9)
  II.   Sinai to Kadesh (Chaps. 10–19)
 III.   Kadesh to Moab (Chaps. 20–36)

I. Israel at Sinai (Chaps. 1-9)

1. The numbering of the people (Chaps. 1, 2)
2. The numbering of the priests and Levities (Chaps. 3, 4)
3. Laws (Chaps. 5, 6)
4. Gifts of the princes (Chap. 7)
5. Consecration of Levites (Chap. 8)
6. The Passover and the guiding cloud (Chap. 9)

For what purpose were the people numbered (1:3)? In preparation for what (13:30)? What was one reason? Why was it necessary that tribal distinction (1:2, 4) be kept in Israel (Heb. 7:14), also family distinction (Luke 1:27)? What tribe was not numbered with the others (1:49)? Why (1:50)? Who were to lead in the march (2:3; 10:14)? Why (Gen. 49:10; Heb. 7:14)? What was the total of the census taken (2:32)? What was the number of the Levites (3:39)?

A distinction should be noted between priests and Levites. The priests were those members of the tribe of Levi descended from Aaron and his sons (3:2–4), and they had charge of priestly functions of the tabernacle, such as sacrificing, ministering in the Holy Place, etc. The Levites, the remaining members of the tribe, were given to Aaron as helpers (3:9) to take care of the tabernacle with its furniture and utensils. All priests were Levites but not all Levites were priests.

In 3:12 we read that the tribe of Levi was set apart to the Lord instead of the first-born of Israel. In patriarchal times, the first-born enjoyed many privileges, one of which was to act as priest of the family. After the slaying of the first-born of the land of Egypt, the Lord commanded that the first-born of the Israelites be sanctified unto Him; i.e., to His service (Ex. 13:12). Now, for reasons that will suggest themselves to the student, the Lord, instead of having the first-born from different tribes serve Him, set apart one particular tribe for that service—Levi. But there were more first-born than Levites. What was then to be done? See 3:46–51. Those above the number of the Levites were to be redeemed from service by the payment of a certain sum. The ceremony is still performed among orthodox Jews of today.

The law of the Nazarite (Chap. 6) sets forth a beautiful type of consecration. A Nazarite (Nazarite comes from a word meaning to separate) was a person who consecrated himself to the Lord with special vows, either temporarily or for life. As examples of the latter class we may mention Samuel (1 Sam. 1:11) and John the Baptist (Luke 1:13–15). The Nazarite drank no wine (typical of abstinence from natural joy), wore his hair long (perhaps willingness to endure reproach for Jehovah, see 1 Cor. 11:14), and was not allowed to touch a dead body, not even of his parents (severance from family ties). The cause of Samson's fall was the breaking of his Nazarite vow (Jud. 13:5; 16:17).

What does the threefold benediction by the priests in Num. 6:24–26 remind you of? (See 2 Cor. 13:14). Notice the beautiful ceremony of the laying of the Israelites' hands on the Levites (8:10). Does Acts 13:2, 3 suggest any resemblance? What new addition to the Passover law was made in chapter 9:1–14? Notice the lesson taught in this connection;

namely that God does not lower His standards but helps men to reach them.

II. **Sinai to Kadesh** (Chaps. 10-19)

1. Beginning of the march (Chap. 10)
2. Murmuring and lusting (Chap. 11)
3. The seventy elders (Chap. 11)
4. Aaron's and Miriam's rebellion (Chap. 12)
5. The spies' report and Israel's unbelief (Chaps. 13–14)
6. Korah's rebellion (Chaps. 16, 17)
7. Ceremonial laws (Chaps. 18, 19)

Did Hobab and his children accompany the children of Israel (Jud. 1:16)? Did they remain with them (1 Sam. 15:6)? What went before the children of Israel (10:33)? What did that represent (Ex. 25:20–22; Josh. 7:6)? What was one of the causes that led to Israel's lusting (11:4; compare Ex. 12:38)? What lesson is there here for us (2 Cor. 6:14)? Who were appointed to assist Moses (11:16, 17)? What does the manifestation of the Spirit in 11:25 remind you of (Acts 19:6)? Was Moses' prayer in verse 29 ever answered (Acts 2:17; 1 Cor. 14:31)? Notice that the quails were not piled two cubits high, as might seem from the hasty reading of 11:31, but they flew that high and so were easily captured.

Notice how contagious was the spirit of murmuring. It affected even Miriam and Aaron. From the fact that Miriam's name is mentioned first in verse 1, and that she was the one who was punished, it seems clear that she was the leader in the rebellion. Since marriage with Gentiles was discouraged by the Law (Gen. 24:3; Deut. 7:3), Miriam had a just cause for complaint. But she failed to take into account the grace of God that can sanctify Gentiles. Some have seen in Moses' action a dispensational and prophetic significance. Rejected by Israel, Moses married a Gentile bride (Acts 15:14). Aaron and Miriam represent those Jews who objected to the union of Jew and Gentile (Acts 11:1–3). The exclusion of Miriam is typical of the temporary rejection of Israel, and her reception into the camp, of their restoration.

Deut. 1:9–22 shows that the command to send out the spies was given in response to the people's request. God's plan was that the people should trust Him in this matter, but seeing the weakness of their faith, He allowed them to have their own way.

Whose name was changed at this time (13:16)? What does a change of name in the Bible usually signify (Gen. 32:28)? What kind of report did the spies bring back (13:25–33)? What effect did the report have on the people? What did they plan to do (14:4)? What was the attitude of the faithless people toward those who really believed God (v. 10)? What does 14:13–19 reveal as to the character of Moses? Notice verse 21. In spite of the people's failure, God's plan would be fulfilled. What was Israel's unbelief the beginning of (14:25)? Notice verse 28. As reward is according to faith, so loss is according to unbelief. Was the sin of the people pardoned (v. 20)? Did that save them from reaping what they had sown because of their unrepentant attitude (14:29, 30)? What happened to the men who brought the evil report (v. 37)? Was the act of the people in 40–45 true obedience? What was it (v. 44)?

In chapter 14:22, the Lord mentions the fact, that up to this time, the people had tempted Him ten times. Look up the following Scriptures and make a list of these temptations: Exodus 14; 15; 16; 16:20, 27; 17; 32; Numbers 11; 12:1; 14

Chapter 15:27–29 deals with sins of ignorance; i.e., sins not committed in the spirit of wilful disobedience. In contrast verse 30 mentions sins committed presumptuously, for which sacrifice does not avail, and the following verses give an illustration of such a sin in the case of a man who gathered sticks on the Sabbath. The severe penalty visited was not for the mere act of gathering sticks, but for the spirit of presumption in which the Law was broken.

Why was it necessary for the Lord to command the Israelites to wear a fringe on their garments (15:37–41) as a visible reminder of His commandments (Psa. 78:11; Jer. 2:32)?

Notice in the case of Korah and his company how the murmuring, begun after the departure from Egypt, has developed into open rebellion. The sin of Korah and his company consisted in rebellion against Moses and Aaron and intrusion into the priestly office. Did Moses attempt to vindicate himself (16:4)? Against whom was Korah really rebelling (v. 11)? Was Korah's accusation true (13)? How was he punished? How were the 250 men punished? What shows the utter hardness of the people's hearts (v. 41)?

Chapter 19 gives an account of the preparation of a water for legal purification. For its typical significance read Heb. 9:13, 14. Its main purpose was for the cleansing of people who had touched dead bodies, which touch brought defilement. This law may have been enacted because of the presence of so many dead after Jehovah's judgment on the rebels, for it is not found in Leviticus.

III. Kadesh to Moab (Chaps. 20-36)

1. Moses' sin (Chap. 20)
2. Death of Miriam and Aaron (Chap. 20)
3. The brazen serpent (Chap. 21)
4. Balaam's error and doctrine (Chaps. 22–25)
5. The numbering of the new generation (Chap. 26)
6. Preparations to enter the land (Chaps. 27–36)

We have come to the end of Israel's thirty-eight years of wandering, and we find them again at Kadesh-barnea; the same place from which they turned back to begin their long journey in the wilderness. That period is almost a blank as far as historical record is concerned. It was simply a time of waiting until the unbelieving generation had died out. They are now ready to enter the land.

In what did Moses' sin consist (20:12; Psa. 106:32, 33)? What does this teach us concerning Moses, in spite of the beauty of his character (James 5:17)?

Though Esau and his brother Jacob became reconciled, the descendants of the former harbored enmity toward Israel, as shown in chapter 20. This enmity was never forgotten (See Psa. 137:7; Ezek. 35:1–5; Obadiah 1:10–14).

What types of the atonement does the brazen serpent suggest to you (John 3:14; Gal. 3:19; Rom. 8:3)?

We now come to the story of Balaam. The fact of his being a prophet teaches us that sometimes God revealed His will to individuals other than Israelites. Melchizedek and Cornelius, both Gentiles, will serve as further examples. It is clear that Balaam's besetting sin was covetousness (2 Peter 2:15). It may be asked why God permitted Balaam to go with the messengers and then was angry at him for so doing (22:20, 22). It was God's perfect will that Balaam refuse to go, but seeing the intenseness of his purpose, He gave His permission, but with this condition, "yet the word which I shall say unto thee, that shalt thou do" (v. 20). Now, reading verses 22, 32 and 35, we infer that Balaam left with the thought in mind of violating that very condition.

Thus far we have had a record of Balaam's **error** (Jude 11), which consisted in the belief that God could not refuse to curse such a sinful people as Israel. But he failed to take into account that which could blot out their sins like a thick cloud—the grace of God. Now in chapter 25 we are given an account of Balaam's **doctrine** (Rev. 2:14), which consisted in teaching Balak to corrupt by immorality, the people which he could not curse by enchantments.

Why was it necessary to re-number the people (26:64, 65)? What do we learn in 26:11 concerning Korah's children? What was Moses' attitude toward the Israelites to the very last (27:15–17)? What was the Lord's estimate of Joshua (v. 18)? With what was he endued (v. 20)? By what ceremony was he inducted into office (v. 23)?

Against whom were the Israelites to go to war (Chap. 31)? Why (Chap. 25)? Who in particular perished in this war (v. 8)? Was his prayer in Num. 23:10 granted?

Some have objected to the wholesale slaughter of the Midianites as being inconsistent with the love of God. But let it be remembered that these people were a moral cancer in the midst of a land that threatened the purity of Israel. Read in Leviticus 18:24–30 and context, the account of the corruption of the nations surrounding Israel, and it will be seen that the action of the Lord in utterly destroying them was as necessary from the standpoint of the natural as the action of a surgeon in amputating a diseased limb.

The 32,000 female children (31:18) were kept alive for domestic service, and not for immoral purposes as some infidels have imagined. Had not Israel been severely punished for impurity (25)? Was not impurity punishable by death (Deut. 22)? Hebrew law permitted a soldier to marry a captive woman but only on condition of observing the legislation made in her favor, designed as far as possible to make immorality impossible (Deut. 21:10–14).

Passing over Chapter 32, recording the choice of land of the two and a half tribes; over 33, containing a summary of Israel's journeys; and 34, recording the borders of each tribe, we come to chapter 35, containing the account of the appointment of cities of refuge. What was the inheritance of the Levites? For whom were the six cities of refuge to be (v. 11, 12)? Where were these cities to be located (v. 14)? How long was the slayer to remain there (v. 25)? Who was excluded from the cities (vv. 20, 21)?

CHAPTER V

DEUTERONOMY

Title. Deuteronomy comes from two Greek words meaning "second law," and is so called from the fact that it records the repetition of the laws given at Sinai.

Theme. Moses has fulfilled his mission. He has led Israel from Egypt to the borders of the Promised Land. Now that the time of his departure is at hand, he reviews before the new generation, in a series of discourses, Israel's past history and upon this review he bases the warnings and exhortations that make Deuteronomy one great exhortatory sermon to Israel. He exhorts them to remember Jehovah's love toward them during the wilderness wanderings, in order that they may rest assured of His continued care of them when they enter Canaan. He admonishes them to observe the Law in order that they might prosper. He reminds them of their past backslidings and rebellions, and warns them of the consequences of future disobedience. The message of Deuteronomy may be summed up in three exhortations: Remember! Obey! Take heed!

Author. Moses

Scope. Two months on the plains of Moab, 1451 BC.

CONTENTS

We shall outline Deuteronomy according to the three exhortations mentioned in our theme.

    I. Remember!—Review of the Wanderings
       (Chaps. 1–4)

   II. Obey!—Review of the Law (Chaps. 5–27)

  III. Take Heed!—Prophecy of Israel's Future
       (Chaps. 28–34)

I. Remember!—Review of Israel's Wanderings (Read Deuteronomy 1-4)

Since the events recorded in the following chapters are simply a repetition for the most part of those given in Numbers, we shall not dwell on them. We may divide the section into two parts:

    1. Moses reviews Israel's wanderings (Chaps. 1–3)

    2. Makes that review a basis for a warning (Chap. 4)

Where do we find Israel at the beginning of this book (1:5)? What prophecy had been partially fulfilled in Israel (v. 10 and Gen. 15:5)? In what one instance was Moses' prayer refused (3:25–28)? What was to be Israel's attitude toward the Word of God (4:2)? What was the Law to Israel (4:6)? Concerning what days does Moses prophesy in 4:25–30? To what book written by himself does Moses indirectly refer (4:32)?

II. Obey!—Review of the Law (Chaps. 5-27)

    1. The Ten Commandments (Chaps. 5–6)

    2. Warnings and exhortations (Chaps. 7–12)

    3. False prophets (Chap. 13)

    4. Ceremonial laws (Chaps. 14–16)

    5. A future king and a future Prophet (Chaps. 17–18)

    6. Civil laws (Chaps. 19–26)

    7. Blessings and cursings of the Law (Chaps. 27)

What was God's earnest desire for His people (5:29)? Will it ever be realized (Ezek. 36:26)? What is the one great commandment of the Law (6:4,

5)? Was Israel chosen because of their greatness or righteousness (7:7; 9:4)? For what two reasons were they chosen (7:8)? What was one of the purposes of God's leading Israel through the wilderness (8:2–5, 16)? What was all that God required of Israel (10:12)? What was to be the difference between Israel's conduct in the wilderness and that in the Land of Promise (12:8)? Where were sacrifices only to be offered (12:13, 14)? Do miracles necessarily prove the genuineness of a prophet (13:1, 2; 2 Thess. 2:9)? What is the test (13:2; Matt. 7:15–23)? What did Moses foresee (17:14–16; compare 1 Sam. 8:5, 10–18)? What great prophecy did Moses utter in 18:15–19? Note that the law of retribution in 19:21 was given to be enforced by the judges and not by ordinary individuals. With what does the review of the Law end (27:26)? What is our relation to it (Gal. 3:13)?

III. Take Heed!—Prophecies of Israel's Future
(Chaps. 28–34)

1. Blessings and cursings (Chap. 28)
2. The Palestinian covenant (Chaps. 29, 30)
3. Moses' last counsels to the priests, Levites and Joshua (Chap. 31)
4. The song of Moses (Chap. 32)
5. The blessing of the tribes (Chap. 33)
6. The death of Moses (34)

Chapter 28, together with Leviticus 26, should be remembered as the two great prophetic chapters of the Pentateuch. Verses 1–14 would have been fulfilled if Israel had been obedient but they will find their ultimate fulfillment during the Millennium. Verses 14–36 were fulfilled in Israel's apostasy under the kings, which culminated in the Babylonian captivity (2 Chron. 36:15–20). Verses 37–68 were fulfilled during the destruction of Jerusalem, 70 AD and the period following (Luke 21:20–24). Josephus, a Jewish general and historian who lived during those days, gives some vivid accounts of the terrible sufferings of the Jews at that time, which indicate how literally the foregoing verses were fulfilled. As a commentary on verse 53, we cite the following incident taken from the history of the siege.

During the period of greatest famine in Jerusalem, a party of armed marauders were wandering through the streets in search of food. They smelled the odor of roasting flesh from a near-by house. Entering, they commanded the woman there to give them food. Whereupon, to their horror, she uncovered the roasted body of her infant! It will be plain to anyone who has some knowledge of the Jewish people how the prophecies of verses 37–68 have been made history.

Chapters 29 and 30 record what is known as the Palestinian covenant; that is, an agreement between the Lord and Israel as to the conditions of their possessing Palestine. It should be carefully noted that there are two covenants which relate to Israel's possession of the land. The first is the Abrahamic covenant (Gen. 17:7, 8). This covenant was **unconditional;** that is, Israel's conduct would not effect its fulfillment. (See Jer. 31:35–37; Rom. 11:26–29). But God saw that Israel would sin, so He put them under another covenant—the Palestinian. This covenant is **conditional** upon Israel's obedience, and enables the Lord to punish them with **temporary** banishment from the land without casting them off **forever**. To use a crude illustration; the Abrahamic covenant was the inheritance laid up for an obedient Israel; the Palestinian covenant was the whip to bring Israel to that place of obedience. Dr. Scofield furnishes an excellent analysis of the last named covenant. It made provision for—

1. Israel's dispersion for disobedience (30:1)
2. Future repentance of Israel (v. 2)
3. The return of the Lord (v. 3)

4. Restoration to Palestine (v. 5)
5. National conversion (v. 6)
6. Judgment of Israel's oppressors (v. 7)
7. National prosperity (v. 9)

How often was the Law to be read to the people (31:10–13)? What did the Lord warn Moses of (31:16)? In view of this, what was Moses to do (vv. 19–21)? What did Moses know (v. 29)?

The song of Moses, contained in chapter 32, may be considered as a summary of the whole book of Deuteronomy. It may be summed up in the three words of our theme—remember, obey, heed. It was written in the form of a song so as to be more easily remembered by the people.

What is said concerning God's character in 32:4? Israel's character (vv. 5, 6)? What country did the Lord make the center of all nations (v. 8)? What is said concerning Jehovah's care of Israel (vv. 10–14)? Was Israel grateful (vv. 15–18)? Who was to provoke Israel to jealousy (v. 21; cf. Rom. 11:11)? How would Jehovah punish them (vv. 22–26)? What would prevent Jehovah from making a full end of them (v. 27)? What was His desire for them (v. 29)? When will He return to them (v. 36)? Who will finally rejoice with Israel (v. 43)? When?

Moses' blessing of the tribes should be compared with that of Jacob found in Genesis 49.

It is possible that Joshua wrote the account of Moses' death found in chapter 34. What is a probable reason why the location of Moses' tomb was never revealed (cf. Num. 21:8 and 2 Kings 18:4)? What other Scripture mentions his burial (Jude 9)? What was his physical condition at death? What did Israel do at Moses' death that they ought to have done during his lifetime (v. 8)? Did ever a prophet arise in Israel like Moses (cf. v. 10 and 18:15)?

JOSHUA

Theme. Israel is now ready to take posession of Canaan, and fulfill their God-given commission to be a witness to the nations of His unity, and a guardian of His word and Law. In the historical books, beginning with Joshua, we shall see whether or not Israel fulfilled their commission. Joshua is the book of victory and possession. It gives us the spectacle of the once rebellious Israel transformed into a disciplined army of warriors, subduing nations, their superiors in numbers and power. The secret of their success is not hard to find—"the Lord fought for them." Taking God's faithfulness as our central thought, we may sum up the message of Joshua in the words of chapter 21:45, "There failed not ought of anything which the Lord had spoken unto the house of Israel; all came to pass."

Author. Joshua. The Talmud says that Joshua wrote all of the book except the last five verses. It was written during Rahab's lifetime (6:25).

Scope. From the death of Moses to the death of Joshua, covering a period of 24 years, from 1451 to 1427 BC.

CONTENTS

I.   **The Land Entered** (Chaps. 1-5)

1. Joshua's charge and commission (Chap. 1)
2. Rahab and the spies (Chap. 2)
3. The Jordan crossed (Chap. 3)
4. Two memorials (Chap. 4)
5. The first Passover in Canaan (Chap. 5)

How much land were the Israelites to possess (1:3)? What spiritual truth does this illustrate (Matt. 19:29)? What was to be Joshua's guide now (1:8)? Note that up to this time the Lord made known His will through visions, dreams and angelic appearances, but now it is through the written Word. What are the two and a half tribes reminded of (1:13–15)? What kind of woman was Rahab (2:1)? What saved her (Heb. 11:31)? Did she do anything difficult to obtain salvation (2:21)? What did Joshua command as a memorial of the crossing of the Jordan (4:3, 9)? What was the effect of the report of Israel's coming upon the Canaanites (5:1)? What did it fulfill (Deut. 2:25)? What change of diet did the Israelites undergo at this time (5:11, 12)? Who was the real leader of Israel's hosts (5:13, 14)? Who was this (Rev. 19:11–16)?

II. **The Land Subdued** (Chaps. 6-12)

1. The conquest of Jericho (Chap. 6)
2. Achan's sin (Chap. 7)
3. Conquest of Ai (Chap. 8)
4. Dealings with the Gibeonites (Chap. 9, 10)
5. Final conquest of the land (Chap. 11, 12)

What does the taking of Jericho teach concerning God's ways of working (1 Cor. 1:26–31)? What warning was given Israel (6:18)? What curse was pronounced at that time (6:26)? Upon whom did it fall (1 Kings 16:34)? To what New Testament characters may we compare Achan (Acts 5)? Who were punished for the sin of one man (7:1)? Is it sometimes out of order to pray (v. 10; cf. Ex. 14:15)? What was at the bottom of Achan's sin (1 Tim. 6:1–10)? What was the symbol of Moses' power (Ex. 10:13)? Of Joshua's power (8:18, 26)? What command of Moses did Joshua fulfill at this time (8:30–35, cf. Deut. 27)? What mistake did Joshua make in his dealings with Gibeon (9:14)? Why were the Gibeonites spared (9:19)? How were they punished (vv. 23–27)?

Note the reference to the conclusion of Joshua's campaign (11:23). How many kings did he conquer (12:24)? What was the secret of his success (10:42)?

III. The Land Divided (Chaps. 13–22)

Since the above heading sums up the contents of the entire section, a detailed outline will be unnecessary.

According to 13:1, what had Israel failed to do (1:3)? What warning did Israel fail to heed? (cf. 13:13; 15:63; 16:10, with Num. 33:55 and Josh. 23:12, 13).

IV. Joshua's Farewell (Chaps. 23, 24)

What did Joshua enjoin upon the elders of Israel (23:6)? What did Joshua foresee (23:13)? What choice does he put before the people (24:15)? What obligation do the people take upon themselves (24:16–18)? From what you know of Israel's history, did they keep their promise? What did Joshua make with the people (v. 25)?

CHAPTER VI

JUDGES

Theme. Joshua is the book of victory; Judges, the book of failure. The verses of chapter 2:7–19 sum up the story of the book. After Joshua's death, the new generation of Israelites made alliances with those nations that the old generation had left in the land, and the result was a lapse into idolatry and immorality. This brought upon them the judgment of God in the form of servitude to those nations which they should have subdued. Upon their crying unto God, a deliverer was sent unto them, during whose lifetime they remained faithful to God but after whose death they again relapsed into their old sins. In the last few chapters of the book, the writer gives us a close-up view of those times of apostasy and anarchy, and explains it all by the fact that "In those days there was no king in Israel; every man did that which was right in his own eyes." The story of the book may be summed up in four words: Sin, Servitude, Sorrow, Salvation.

Author. According to Jewish tradition the author was Samuel.

Scope. It covers the period between the death of Joshua and the judgeship of Samuel.

CONTENTS

I. **The Period After Joshua** (Chaps. 1 to 3:4)

1. The incomplete victory of the tribes (Chap. 1)
2. Visit of the angel (Chaps. 2:1–5)
3. Review of events leading up to Israel's apostasy (Chaps. 2:6 to 3:4)

Notice that chapter 1 records that which was the beginning of Israel's fall—their failure to conquer the Canaanites, and their subsequent alliance with them (2:12). Though contrary to His will that the Canaanites dwell in the same land with Israel, what use does the Lord make of them (2:21–23)? What else did He use for the same purpose (Deut. 8:2–16)?

II. **Israel's Apostasies, Captivities, and Deliverances** (Chaps. 3:5 to 16:31)

Let the student make a list of all the judges, giving the following facts connected with each:

1. From whom did he deliver Israel?
2. How long was he in office?
3. What were the important facts concerning him?

Note that there were twelve judges (excluding Abimelech who was a usurper). What does that suggest to you (Matt. 19:28; Isa. 1:26)? Three important facts concerning the judges should be noted: they were called of God, endued with special power, and most of them belonged to that class described by Paul as "the weak things of the world . . . the base things of the world" (1 Cor. 1:27, 28).

Jael's action in killing Sisera, and Deborah's praise of the same, has called forth criticism from some quarters. Two things should be taken into consideration here. First, that although Deborah and Barak glorify the act, the Bible does not endorse or commend it; it simply records the fact. On the other hand, we must take into account the fact that the age in which Jael lived differed from ours in regard to customs and standards. We quote from an English commentator:

> Jael by her righteous and courageous act saved her life, defended the honor of her absent husband, her own honor, and that of many hundreds of her sex (5:30). By going into the woman's tent, Sisera was guilty of a most cruel action and it was a very base return for the hospitality and kindness shown to him. He well knew that the Desert Law condemned to death a woman into whose part of the tent a man entered. She could only save herself by, if possible, putting him to death. Such was the Law of the Desert; and Jael was a daughter of the Desert, and not of Israel.

How did the angel of the Lord address Gideon (6:12)? Was that Gideon's estimate of himself (6:15)? Was Gideon conscious of unbelief in asking for a sign (6:39)? Why did God want to deliver Israel with only a few men (7:2)? What law does 7:3 refer to (Deut. 20:8)? What can be said concerning the weapons of Gideon's band (2 Cor. 10:4, 5; Zech. 4:6).

We now come to a question which can hardly be passed in a study of the book of Judges; namely, Did Jephthah really sacrifice his daughter? Since scholars are divided on the question, we can but give what each side has to say on the subject and let the student judge for himself. Some believe, that since human sacrifices were forbidden by law (Lev. 18:21; 20:2–5), the offering of Jephthah's daughter must have taken the form of a dedication of the girl to perpetual virginity (11:36–40). Others believe that he actually sacrificed his daughter in the conscientious belief that he was bound by his oath (vv. 31, 35, 39).

Who was it that Samson's parents saw (13:17, 18, 22; cf. Gen. 32:29, 30)? What was Samson from his birth (13:4, 5)? Whom did he resemble in this respect (Luke 1:13–15)? Was he to be separated unto the Lord

(13:5)? Did he always remain separated (14:1–3)? What was the secret of his strength (13:25)? Did he always walk according to the Spirit (16:1–24)? How strong was he (14:5–7)? How weak was he (16:1–17)? What caused his fall (16:19; 13:5)?

III. Israel's Anarchy (Chaps. 17-21)

1. Anarchy in religious life (17, 18)
2. Anarchy in moral life (19)
3. Anarchy in national life (20, 21)

The first half of the book of Judges gives us a short sketch of some of Israel's apostasies during the 450 years the judges ruled. Chapters 17 to 21 give us a close-up view of one of those periods. The last verse of the book offers an explanation for the terrible conditions that prevailed during that time.

RUTH

Theme. Judges gave us a very dark picture of Israel as seen from the national viewpoint; Ruth gives us a bright picture of that period as seen in the faithfulness and in the beauty of character of certain individuals. The story is one of the most beautiful in the Bible, and is doubly interesting from the fact that its heroine is a Gentile. The very last word in the book—David—will reveal its chief value. Its purpose is to trace the descent of David, the progenitor of the Messiah. The whole book has its climax in the genealogy found in the last chapter.

Author. Jewish tradition assigns the authorship to Samuel.

Scope. The book covers a period of ten years probably during the time of Gideon.

CONTENTS

We shall use the outline given by Dr. Scofield.

I.   **Ruth Deciding** (Chaps. 1)

When did the events recorded in this book take place (1:1)? Ought there to have been a famine at this time (Deut. 28:1–14)? If Elimelech had trusted God would he have gone to Moab (Ps. 37:3)? What happened to the family in Moab (vv. 3, 4)? What was Ruth's decision (vv. 16, 17)?

II. **Ruth Serving** (Chaps. 2)

Chapter 2:3 says that Ruth happened to light on a field belonging to Boaz, a kinsman of Elimelech. Subsequent events will show that this happening was divinely ordained. Notice Boaz' prophetic blessing of Ruth (2:12).

III. **Ruth Resting** (Chaps. 3)

This chapter calls for an explanation of some Jewish laws and customs. Elimelech, through poverty, had lost his property. According to Jewish law, the property could be redeemed by a kinsman of the former owner (Lev. 25:25). Boaz, as a kinsman of Elimelech had this right. Another law required that if a man died childless, his brother should marry the widow (Deut. 25:5–10). It seems, however, that custom had decided, in the course of time, that in the absence of a brother-in-law, the duty should devolve on the nearest kinsman. Naomi, since she was the widow of Elimelech, and since she had no children, had a claim on Boaz. This claim she gave over to Ruth. Ruth is sent to Boaz, and by the symbolic act of lying at his feet, reminded him of the duty owed to his deceased kinsman (3:7–9). Boaz, though willing to marry Ruth, reminded her that there was a nearer relative than he, who would have first claim.

IV. Ruth Rewarded (Chap. 4)

The next morning Boaz takes witnesses and offers the right of the redemption of Naomi's property to his kinsman, at the same time reminding him that if he bought the property, he would have to marry Ruth. This he refuses to do leaving Boaz free to marry Ruth.

Chapter 4:18, 22 though seemingly an uninteresting list of names, is the climax to which the book leads, for it reveals the purpose of its writing—to show the descent of David, the progenitor of the Messiah (cf. Matt. 1:3–6).

CHAPTER VII

FIRST SAMUEL

Theme. The book of Samuel is a transition book. It is the record of the passing of the government of Israel by judges to the government by kings and of the passing from the rule of God, the invisible king—which made them unlike other nations—to the rule of a visible king which made them like other nations. "The book of Samuel is a history with the personal attraction of biography added. The contents may be grouped around three persons: Samuel, a patriot and judge with lowly consecrated heart, obediently serving God; Saul, a selfish, wayward, jealous king, faulty and unfaithful in allegiance to his God; David "a man after God's own heart, the sweet singer of Israel, a man of prayer and praise, tested, disciplined, persecuted, and finally crowned monarch of all Israel."

Author. Samuel is generally supposed to have written the book as far as chapter 24; and from the fact that the prophets Nathan and Gad are mentioned with Samuel in 1 Chron. 29:29, as writers of the events of David's life, it is considered that they were the authors of the remaining chapters.

Scope. From the birth of Samuel to the death of Saul, covering a period of 115 years from about 1171 BC to 1056 BC.

CONTENTS

The contents of the Book of Samuel may be grouped around three persons: Samuel, Saul and David.

I.   Concerning Samuel (Chaps. 1–7)
II. Concerning Saul (Chaps. 8–15)
III. Concerning David (Chaps. 16–31)

I. Concerning Samuel (Chaps. 1-7)

1. The birth of Samuel (Chap. 1 to 2:11)
2. The call of Samuel (Chaps. 2:12 to 3)
3. The taking of the ark (Chaps. 4, 5)
4. The return of the ark (Chaps. 6, 7)

Where was the place of worship at this time of Israel's history (1:3)? When did Jerusalem become the place of worship (2 Sam. 5:6–9)? What place did Hannah hold in her husband's heart (v. 8)? What was her grief? What did it mean in those days for a Jewish woman to be without children (Gen. 30:23; Luke 1:25)? What kind of child did Hannah request from the Lord (v. 11)? What did she promise he should be (v. 11, compare Numbers ch. 6)? Whom does she resemble in this respect (Luke 1:13–15)? Why was Samuel so called (v. 20)? Did Hannah fulfill her vow (1:24–28)? What did Jehovah's kindness to her inspire (2:1–10)? What Israelitish woman uttered similar words under like circumstances (Luke 1:46–55)?

Is it possible for persons to be in the ministry and yet be sinful (2:12)? What is said concerning Eli's sons? How did these young men injure the Lord's cause (2:17)? Was Hannah well repaid for her sacrifice (2:21)? What warning was given Eli (2:27–36)? What was the condition of revelation in those days (3:1)? What must have been the condition of the people in consequence (Prov. 29:18; Ps. 74:9; Amos 8:11)? What shows that God can reveal His will to a little child? How did the Lord confirm Samuel's call (3:19, 20)? Samuel was the first of the line of writing prophets (Acts 3:24; 13:20; 1 Sam. 3:20). After the priesthood had failed, Samuel became the spiritual leader of the people and the mediator between them and God.

Chapters 4, 5 record the taking of the ark. The ark was a symbol of the presence of the glory of the Lord (Num. 14:43, 44; Josh 3:6; 1 Sam. 14:18, 19; Ps. 132:8). It went before the Israelites in their wilderness wanderings and sometimes before the army in time of war (Josh. 3:6). It was before the ark that the leaders sought the will of the Lord (Ex. 25:22; Josh. 7:6–9; Jud. 20:27). Israel, in their backslidden condition, made a superstitious use of this piece of sacred furniture, thinking that the mere formal use of it would bring victory. They trusted in "it" instead of the Lord's power of which it was a symbol (4:3). Their great shout in the camp was the result of mere natural enthusiasm.

While the ark brought blessing to God's people, what did it bring to God's enemies (Chap. 5)? What light did the wise men of the Philistines have on divine healing (6:3–6)? With what history were they acquainted (6:6)? What was the effect on the Israelites of seeing the ark returning (6:13)? Of what act of profanation were the people guilty (6:19, compare Num. 4:5, 15)? Where was the ark then taken? Over what did the Israelites lament (7:2)? What did Samuel tell them to do (7:3)? Of what is the act of the Israelites mentioned (7:6) typical (Ps. 62:8)? What prominence is given to prayer in this chapter (7:5, 8, 9)? Notice that Samuel takes upon himself the office of priest by sacrificing (7:9). Though only the priests were allowed to sacrifice, the Lord made special dispensation in Samuel's favor, because of the failure of the priesthood. What followed Israel's repentance (7:10–14)?

II. Concerning Saul (Chaps. 8-15)

1. Israel demands a king. (Chap. 8)
2. Saul chosen and anointed (Chaps. 9, 10)

3. Saul's first victory (Chap. 11)
4. Samuel's proclamation of the kingdom (Chap. 12)
5. Saul's rejection (Chaps. 13–15)

Chapter 8 records the desire of Israel for a king. What was the reason for desiring a king (8:5)? What was God's plan for the nation (Deut. 14:2; Num. 23:9)? What gave the people an excuse for demanding a king (8:3–5)? How closely is God identified with His servants (8:7)? Did God let the people have their own way? What kind of king did the Lord say they would have (8:11–17)? Who had foreseen that Israel would desire a king (Deut. 17:14–20)? Did the Lord's description of their future king discourage the people (8:19, 20)? What did the Lord then do (Ps. 106:15)?

What was Samuel's reputation among the people (9:6)? What was a prophet originally called (9:9)? How close to God did Samuel live (9:15)? What signs were given to confirm Saul's faith (10:1–8)? Notice here the existence of a school of prophets of which Samuel was probably the head (10:5, 10). Chapter 10:6–9 does not teach that Saul was regenerated. It does indeed state that the Lord gave Saul a new heart, but that simply means that He imparted unto him the necessary qualifications for his office. He gave him the heart of a king. Saul's action in hiding himself among the stuff has been interpreted as indicating modesty on his part. But it was modesty displayed at the wrong time. "It is as great a sin to urge modesty and keep in the background when God calls to the foreground as it is to go to the front when God's appointment is in the rear." Were all the people in favor of Saul (10:27)? How did he show his wisdom (10:27)? What established Saul's popularity (11:11–13)? Though Israel had rejected Jehovah, did He utterly forsake them (12:14, 22)? As what did Samuel consider neglect of intercessory prayer (12:23)?

Chapter 13 records Saul's sin—intruding into the priest's office. This was in flagrant violation of Num. 3:10, 38. What excuse did he offer (v. 12)? What did he lose through his disobedience (13:13)? What was made known to Saul (13:14)?

What act of disobedience sealed Saul's fate (15:1–9)? What excuse did Saul offer (vv. 20, 21)? What principle did Samuel lay down in 15:22? Was Saul's repentance really sincere (Compare v. 25 and 30)? What were Samuel's feelings on Saul's rejection (15:35)? The Lord's feelings?

III. Concerning David (Chaps. 16–31)

1. David anointed king (Chap. 16)
2. David's victory over Goliath (Chap. 17)
3. David's persecutions and wanderings (Chaps. 18–30)
4. The death of Saul (Chap. 31)

By what was Samuel judging the fitness of a person to become king (16:6)? How does the Lord judge (16:7)? What happened after David's anointing (16:13)? Of what event was this typical (Matt. 3:16, 17)?

Chapter 16:14 seems to present a difficulty. We read that the Spirit of the Lord departed from Saul and that an evil spirit from the Lord troubled him. It has been asked, Does God send evil spirits to men? In explanation of this we quote from Dr. Torrey:

> What is meant by 'evil spirit'? The context clearly shows. It was a spirit of discontent, unrest, depression.
>
> The circumstances were these: Saul had proved untrue to God. He had deliberately disobeyed God, and consequently God had withdrawn His Spirit from him, and a spirit of worry and discontent came upon him.

This was not an unkind act on God's part. There was nothing kinder that God could have done. It is one of the most merciful provisions of our heavenly Father that when we disobey Him and wander from Him He makes us unhappy and discontented in our sin. If God should leave us to continue to be happy in our sin, it would be the unkindest thing He could do, but God in His great mercy will win every sinner possible back to Himself, and if we sin, God, for our highest good sends us unrest and deep depression in our sin. If we make right use of this spirit of depression that God sends us it brings us back to God and to the joy of the Holy Ghost. Saul made the wrong use of it. Instead of allowing the unrest of his heart to bring him to repentance he allowed it to embitter his soul against the one whom God had favored. The sending of the spirit was an act of mercy on God's part. The misuse of this act of mercy resulted in Saul's undoing.

Students have been puzzled that Saul should not have recognized David after his victory over Goliath when he had just sent him forth (17:55–58). Mr. Parrot, a missionary to Madagascar, explains this difficulty by describing a custom of that country. In Madagascar when "a man has performed some exploit, the cry is not 'Who is this?' but, 'Whose son is he?' the glory passing to the one who fathered him. Further, the Malagasy custom is to feign ignorance of the parentage the better to express surprise."

Who befriended David at this time (18:1)? What caused Saul's jealousy (18:6, 7)? Why did Saul fear him (18:12)? How popular was David with Israel (18:16)? How did Saul attempt to take David's life (18:20–30; 19:1–17)? How did the Lord protect David (19:18–24)? Where did David flee (19:18)? What was at the root of Saul's enmity toward David (20:31)?

Let the student make a list of the places where David went during his wanderings, noting what occurred at each place.

We have been reading the account of the wanderings and persecutions of him who had been anointed king over Israel. What were his feelings during that time? His religious experiences? The reading of the following psalms, referring to this period of his life, will answer those questions. Let the student read them: Psalm 59, compare 1 Sam. 19:11; Psalm 56, compare 1 Sam. 21:10, 11; Psalm 34, compare 1 Sam. 21:13; Psalm 57, compare 1 Sam. 22:1; Psalm 52, compare 1 Sam. 22:9; Psalm 54, compare 1 Sam. 23:19.

CHAPTER VIII

SECOND SAMUEL

Theme.

The whole book centers around the figure of David; there is none other of sufficient importance to draw off the attention. It is God's portrait of His anointed to which our eyes are directed. It is the picture of the man after God's own heart that we are called upon to study. And we begin our study with the question: What is there about David to merit so honorable a title? He is not pointed out to us from a distance that we may gaze at the king set upon lofty eminence, surrounded by all the insignia of royalty, but we are invited to a close acquaintance with the man. We see him, not only upon the throne but in the home. We watch him in his deepest sorrows, as well as in the hour of his greatest triumphs; we hear his prayers and his praises, his righteous indignation, his words of kindness, tenderness and generosity. We are witnesses of his sin and his repentance, of his moments of impatience, of his kingly dignity, and the whole picture, in spite of its occasional dark shadows, shows us a man in whose life God really was first, and to whom above all else he was a glorious reality—a man, in short, who was deeply conscious of his own weakness, failure and sin, but who knew God and trusted Him with his whole heart. —Markham.

Author. The events recorded in the book of 2 Samuel were probably added to Samuel's book (1 Chron. 29:29) by Nathan or Gad. In the original Hebrew, 1 and 2 Samuel formed one book. They were divided by the Septuagint translators (about

285 BC) when they translated the Old Testament into the Greek language.

Scope. From the death of Saul to the purchase of the temple site, covering a period of 37 years.

CONTENTS

I. David's Rise (Chaps. 1-10)

  1. The death of Saul (Chap. 1)
  2. David becomes king over all Israel (Chaps. 2–5)
  3. The ark brought to Jerusalem (Chap. 6)
  4. The Davidic covenant (Chap. 7)
  5. David's conquests (Chaps. 8–10)

It is believed by scholars that the story of the Amalekite (2 Sam. 1:4–10) was fabrication. His object in coming to David with the news of Saul's death was to find favor in his sight. He imagined that the king would be pleased at the news of the death of his enemy. David, seeing the evil motive of the young man, justly punished him. In thus doing, David acted on the principle that he had followed all through his dealings with Saul; namely, reverence for the Lord's anointed. He wished to avoid all appearances of being accessory to the death of Saul.

Which was the first tribe to recognize David as king (2:1–4)? How did the men of Jabesh-gilead show kindness to Saul (1 Sam. 31:11–13; 2 Sam. 2:4–7)? Who instigated war between Judah and the eleven tribes (2:8–11)? What was the outcome of the war (3:1)? Who made a league with David at this time (3:12–26)? What is revealed concerning Joab's character in chapter 3? What was David's attitude toward Joab's murder of Abner? Notice David's continued faithfulness to Saul and his house (chapter 4) Where and when was David appointed king over all Israel (Chapter 5)? What city became the capital of the kingdom at this time (5:6–9)? Who built David a home at this time (5:11)? What Psalm did David compose on that occasion (Ps. 30)?

The bringing up of the ark was a laudable act on David's part, but the manner of carrying it was in violation of the Law of God. The ark, instead of being carried on a cart should have been borne by the priests (Num. 4:14, 15; 7:9). Where was the ark taken after this (6:10, 11)? What did its presence bring to that family? Was David's conduct before the ark very dignified? Who took exception to it? With what did she reproach David (v. 20)? With what words did David justify his conduct (v. 21)? What was the result of Michal's criticism of David (v. 23)?

What did David purpose to do (7:1–3)? Who encouraged him in this? Was it however God's will that David should build the temple (1 Chron. 22:8)?

Chapter 7:8–17 records God's making of a covenant with David, whereby He promises to him and his descendants the throne and kingdom forever. We quote from Dr. Scofield:

> This covenant, upon which the glorious kingdom of Christ 'of the seed of David according to the flesh' is to be founded, secures:
>
> 1. A Davidic "house"; i.e., posterity, family.
> 2. A "throne"; i.e., royal authority.
> 3. A kingdom; i.e., a sphere of rule.
> 4. In perpetuity; "forever."
> 5. And this fourfold covenant has but one condition; disobedience in the Davidic family is to be visited with chastisement but not to the abrogation of the covenant (2 Sam. 7:15; Ps. 89:20–37; Isa. 55:3). Chastisement fell; first in the division of the kingdom under Rehoboam, and finally in the

captivities (2 Kings 25:1–7). Since that time but one king of the Davidic family has been crowned and He was crowned with thorns. But the Davidic covenant confirmed to David by the oath of Jehovah and renewed to Mary by the angel Gabriel is immutable (Ps. 89:30–37), and the Lord God will yet give to that thorn-crowned One "the throne of His father David" (Luke 1:31–33; Acts 2:29–32).

Notice David's beautiful prayer of thanksgiving after the making of this covenant (7:18–29).

How did David fully establish his kingdom (Chap. 8)? Make a list of the nations he subdued. How does David again show his kindness to Saul's family (Chap. 9)?

II. David's Fall (Chaps. 11-21)

    1. David's great sin (Chaps. 11, 12)
    2. Absalom's rebellion (Chaps. 13–20)
Read Psalm 51.

Nathan's saying that David had given occasion for the enemies of the Lord to blaspheme (12:14), has found fulfillment in the sneers of infidels who scoff at the fact of David's being called "a man after God's own heart." That David was a man after God's own heart does not mean that he was faultless, but it does mean that he was a man in whose heart there was an earnest desire to do God's will and seek His righteousness, in contrast to Saul, who was always seeking his own way. David committed the foulest of sins yet, with a true sense of Jehovah's righteousness and a sense of his own guilt, he repented in sackcloth and ashes. There are many important lessons we may learn from David's sin:

    1. However strong and spiritual a man may be, if he gets his eyes off God, he is liable to fall.

    2. The recording in plain terms of the sin of Israel's greatest hero without any attempt to whitewash it, is a strong proof of the divine origin of the

Bible. The natural thing to have done would be to draw a veil over this unpleasant event (Chap. 12:12).

3. God's grace can pardon the blackest of sins if there is true repentance (12:13).

4. Whatever a man sows that will he reap. The child of David's sinful union died. His two sons followed him in adultery and one committed murder.

5. God will not for a moment condone sin even on the part of His best beloved children.

It was not long after his incident that David continued to reap what he had sown. His son Amnon committed an act of immorality which led to his murder by Absalom (Chap. 13). David loved his son, but a dread of public opinion had made him hesitate to recall him from the banishment to which he had been sentenced. Joab, knowing the struggle that was taking place in the king's heart, between affection and duty, resorted to a stratagem described in chapter 14. The wise woman he employed, in a skillful speech, obtained a pledge from the king that her son, who had supposedly slain his brother, would be pardoned. She then insinuated that in pardoning Absalom, he would be doing no more than he had done for her, and there could be no charge of partiality against him. The scheme was successful. However, subsequent events prove that David had acted unwisely in pardoning Absalom for his son rebelled against him.

David's prompt decision to leave Jerusalem and place the Jordan between him and the rebels, was the action of a skillful soldier. In connection with David's flight, Psalm 3 should be read.

Notice David's patience and humility in the face of Shimei's insult. He sees the hand of God in everything (16:5–12).

Ahithophel counsels Absalom to commit an act which would cut off all hope of reconciliation with his father, and which would compel every one in Israel to show his colors (16:21–23). This act was a fulfillment of 2 Sam. 12:12. Ahithophel then advises Absalom to take a small force and capture his father before he could gather a large army. Hushai defeated this counsel by suggesting that Absalom make a general mobilization of his whole army. This would give David time to pass over the Jordan and gather a large army. Ahithophel, foreseeing David's victory, and his own disgrace, committed suicide.

Joab's insolent reproof of David shows that he had no love for him (19:1–7). At heart he was a rebel. His having murdered Absalom had turned David completely against him (19:13, compare 1 Kings 2:5).

> This chapter (19) as a mirror, exhibits some sad facts. David seems to have forgotten the use and meaning of prayer. Amid the incessant movement of this chapter it is not once mentioned that 'David enquired of the Lord.' The result was that he allowed selfish and excessive affection for his rebellious son to smother the affection which he should have shown for his brave and faithful soldiers; he pardoned Shimei, swearing to him by Jehovah—an oath which he should not have taken (1 Kings 2:8, 9)—when he ought to have judged him; he condemned Mephibosheth when he should have done him justice; he rewarded Zeba when he should have punished him; and he hastened to Jerusalem without giving time for the chiefs and soldiers of the Northern tribes to assist in the restoration, thus occasioning the bloodshed and misery that followed in the next chapter.

What tribe should have been the first to welcome David back (19:11)? Why (v. 12)? Will the time ever come when Israel and Judah will welcome David's Son (Zech. 12:10; Matt. 23:39)? Who conducted David back to the city (19:40)? What did David's preferment of the tribe of Judah cause (19:41–20:1, 2)?

Of what was this division between Judah and Israel the beginning (1 Kings 12:16–24)? What crime did Joab add to his record at this time (Chap. 20)?

III. David's Later Years (Chaps. 21-23)

1. The three years of famine (Chap. 21)
2. David's song (Chap. 22)
3. David's last words (Chap. 23)
4. David's sin in numbering the people (Chap. 24)

What was the cause of the famine mentioned in Chapter 21 (Compare Josh. Chap. 9)? What penalty did Saul's family pay for the violation of this oath?

Chapter 22 has been called by Spurgeon "The grateful retrospect." Toward the close of his life, David looks back on the vicissitudes and trials of the past and gratefully acknowledges Jehovah's grace and faithfulness.

The first seven verses of chapter 23 record the last words of David. In this connection, Psalm 72 should be read, the last verse of which seems to indicate that it was David's last prayer. What three things are said concerning David in verse 1? What did David claim in verse 2? Who bore witness to this (Matt. 22:43)? What did David say was God's ideal of a ruler (vv. 3, 4)? Did David feel that he and his house had lived up to this standard (v. 5)? Though David had experienced many troubles and failures, what fact comforted him (v. 5)? What does he say concerning his enemies (vv. 6, 7)? The remainder of the chapter gives a list of David's mighty men and their exploits. Verses 16, 17 give us a glimpse of the devotion of these men toward David, and his appreciation of their valor.

Chapter 24 records David's sin in numbering the people. A comparison with 1 Chronicles 21:1–6 shows that it was Satan who instigated this.

God, though He cannot tempt man (James 1:13), is frequently described in Scripture as doing what He merely permits to be done, and so, in this case, He permitted Satan to tempt David. Satan was the active mover, while God only withdrew His supporting grace, and the great tempter prevailed against the king. The order was given by Joab who, though not generally restrained by scruples, did not fail to represent in strong terms (1 Chron. 21:3) the sin and danger of this measure, and used every argument to dissuade the king from his purpose. . . . The fact of numbering the people was not in itself sinful; for Moses did it by the express authority of God. But David acted not only independently of such order or sanction, but from motives unworthy of the delegated king of Israel; from pride and vainglory, from self-confidence and lack of trust in God, and above all, from ambitious designs of conquest, in furtherance of which he was determined to force the people into military service and to ascertain whether he could muster an army sufficient for the magnitude of the enterprise he contemplated. It was a breach of the constitution, an infringement of the liberties of the people, and opposed to that Divine policy which required that Israel should continue a separate nation. —Jamieson, Fausset and Brown.

CHAPTER IX

FIRST KINGS

Theme. In 1 and 2 Samuel we read how the Jewish nation demanded a king in order that they might be like the other nations. Though contrary to His perfect will, God granted their request. In this book we learn how Israel fared under the kings. Though many righteous kings ruled, the history of most of them is one of misrule and iniquity. In accordance with His promise in 1 Samuel 12:18–24, the Lord did not fail to bless His people as long as they sought Him, but, on the other hand He never failed to punish them when they departed from Him.

Author. The human author is unknown. It is believed that Jeremiah compiled the records made by Nathan and Gad (1 Chron. 29:29) and others.

Scope. From the death of David to the reign of Jehoram over Israel, covering a period of 118 years from 1015–897 BC.

CONTENTS

I.   The Establishment of Solomon's Kingdom

(Chaps. 1, 2)

1. Adonijah's plot (1:1–38)
2. Solomon appointed by David (1:39–53)
3. The death of David (2:1–11)
4. Solomon's accession (2:12–46)

What was David's physical condition at this time? Who attempted to seize the kingdom? What should have been a warning to him (2 Sam. 15:1–6)? Who were his accomplices? How was the plot foiled? Why could not Adonijah become king (1 Chron. 22:9, 10)?

Concerning David's last charge to Solomon (2:1–9) we quote from Bahr's commentary:

> The special directions which refer to individual persons, David communicates, not as a private man, but as king of Israel. Joab's double murder had gone fully unpunished. At the time of its commission, David was not in a condition to be able to punish him; but he felt the full weight of his deed, and in horror of it, uttered an imprecation against Joab (2 Sam. 3:29). In the eyes of the people, nevertheless, the non-punishment must have been regarded as an insult against the law and righteousness, the charge of which devolved upon the king. It was a stain upon his reign not yet blotted out. Even on his deathbed he cannot think otherwise than it is his duty, as that of a supreme judge, to deliver to his successor a definite direction about it. It lay upon his conscience, and he desired that the stain somehow ("Do according to thy wisdom") should be removed. Moreover, Joab's participation in Adonijah's revolt must have appeared as dangerous for the throne of Solomon. As the punishment of Joab was to him a matter of conscience, so also was Barzillai's compensation. What Barzillai had done, he had done for him as King, as the anointed of Jehovah. Such fidelity and devotion to the reigning house, ought to be publicly requited, and to be recognized in honorable remembrance after the death of the king. In direct contrast to the action of Barzillai was that of Shimei. He did not curse David as a private person, but he cursed him with the heaviest curse as the anointed of Jehovah, and therein Jehovah Himself indirectly. For blasphemy against the king was on the same level as blasphemy against God (1 Kings 21:10). Both were punished with death

(Lev. 24:14; Ex. 22:28), hence Abishai thought that Shimei should be put to death (2 Samuel 19:21) But David wished on the day when God had showed him great mercy, to show mercy himself, and on that account saved his life. But it was no small matter to allow the miscreant to spend his life near him (no banishment was talked of). And to permit him to spend his days quietly under the following reign (which had never been promised him) would have been a kindness that might have been greatly abused as a precedent of unpunished crimes. In fact, Shimei was a dangerous man, capable of repeating what he had done to David. As for the rest, David left Solomon to choose the manner and time of his punishment only he was not to go unpunished.

II. **Solomon's Reign** (Chaps. 3–11)

1. Solomon's wisdom (Chaps. 3, 4)
2. The building of the temple (Chaps. 5–7)
3. The dedication of the temple (Chap. 8)
4. Solomon's glory and fame (Chaps. 9, 10)
5. Solomon's fall (Chap. 11)

Whom did Solomon marry? Where did Solomon and the people sacrifice for want of a sanctuary (3:2–4)? What request did Solomon make at this time (3:9)? What else did the Lord give besides that for which he asked? What Scripture does that illustrate (Eph. 3:20)? What incident illustrating Solomon's wisdom is given? What was the condition of Israel and Judah during Solomon's reign (4:20, 24, 25)? What were the boundaries of Solomon's dominions (4:21, 24)?

Who supplied Solomon with materials to build the temple? In what year after Israel's departure from Egypt was the building of the temple begun? What message came to Solomon at this time (6:11–13)? How long did it take to build the temple

(6:38)? How long did it take Solomon to build his own house? What was done after the temple was completed (8:1–19)? What did the ark contain? How did God manifest His presence at this time? Notice carefully Solomon's sermon (8:12–21); Solomon's prayer of dedication (8:22–53); Solomon's blessing of the people (8:54–61). How was the dedication celebrated (8:62–66)? When was Solomon's prayer answered (9:1–9)? What choice did the Lord lay before Solomon and his people (9:4–9)? What did Israel ultimately choose? Describe Solomon's activities (9:10–28). Describe his wealth (10:1–29). Who caused Solomon's downfall (11:1, 2)? What did they lead him into (11:5–8)? How did God say He would punish him (11:11)? When would that take place (11:12)? How much of his kingdom would be left? What prophet is introduced here (11:29)? What opportunity was presented Jeroboam (11:38)?

III. The Disruption and Decline of the Kingdom (Chaps. 12-22)

The most profitable way to study this section will be for the student to make a list of the kings of Judah and Israel, briefly noting the following facts: the character of the king; the length of his reign; the names of the prophets mentioned in connection with his reign; the principal events of his reign. For example:

Judah	Israel
Rehoboam	Jeroboam
Foolish and unjust; reigned 17 years; kingdom divided; people commit idolatry; invasion by king of Egypt.	Idolatrous, etc.

The following list of kings of Judah and Israel, arranged as far as possible in chronological order will guide the student.

Judah	Israel
Rehoboam	Jeroboam
Abijam	
Asa	Nadab
	Baasha
	Elah
	Zimri
	Omri
Jehoshaphat	Ahab
Jehoram	Ahaziah

What petition did the elders of the people bring to Rehoboam? In spite of the outward prosperity of Solomon's reign, what was the condition of the people (12:4)? What showed Rehoboam's foolishness? What did he lose by it? Had there already been the beginning of a breach between Judah and Israel (2 Sam. 2:8–11; 19:41 to 20:1, 2)? What did Rehoboam attempt to do to prevent the secession of the other tribes? What restrained him?

What did Jeroboam fear (12:26)? What did he do to prevent this (12:27, 28)? Did he at first wish to entirely destroy the worship of Jehovah, or did he wish to conduct it in another way? What suggested his setting up of the golden calves (Ex. 32:1–4)? Where did he set these? What commandment did he break concerning the priesthood? Concerning the feasts? Who denounced his sin? (13:1, 2)? Whose birth, 350 years before, did he prophesy (Compare 2 Kings 23:15)? What Scripture does the disobedience of the man of God illustrate (Compare 13:18 and Gal. 1:8, 9)? What judgment was pronounced upon Jeroboam? What prophecy concerning Israel was uttered (14:15, 16)?

Let us notice the main events of the ministry of Elijah. In order to give a complete account of his life, we shall draw from 2 Kings.

1. His message to Ahab (17:1)
2. His flight to the brook Cherith (17:2–7)
3. Fed by the widow of Zarephath. Raises her son from the dead (17:8–24)
4. His contest with the priests of Baal on Mt. Carmel (Chap. 18)
5. His flight to Mt. Sinai before Jezebel (19:1–18)
6. The call of Elisha
7. His denunciation of Ahab for the murder of Naboth (21:17–29)
8. His message to Ahaziah (2 Kings 1:3–16)
9. His translation (2 Kings 2:1–11)

Elijah and John the Baptist are mentioned together in the New Testament, the latter as fulfilling the ministry of the former in relation to Messiah's first advent (Luke 1:17; Matt. 17:10–13). Elijah is the John the Baptist of the Old Testament, and John the Baptist is the Elijah of the New Testament. Their ministries yield an interesting comparison.

1. Both ministered in times when Israel had departed from the true spiritual worship of God.
2. They resembled each other in appearance (2 Kings 1:8; Matt. 3:4).
3. Both preached national repentance (1 Kings 18:21; Matt. 3:2).
4. Both rebuked wicked kings (1 Kings 18:18; Matt. 14:3, 4).
5. Both were persecuted by wicked queens (1 Kings 19:1; Matt. 14:8).

6. Elijah's sacrifice on Mt. Carmel, and John's baptism marked a time of national repentance.
7. Elisha, Elijah's successor, received his power for service at the Jordan; Jesus, John's successor, received the anointing of the Spirit in the same river.
8. Both, towards the close of their ministry, yielded to discouragement (1 Kings 19:4; Matt. 11:2–6).

CHAPTER X

SECOND KINGS

Theme. The second book of Kings is a continuation of the story of the downfall of Judah and Israel, culminating in the captivity of both. There is the same story of failure on the part of king and people, a story of backsliding and idolatry. Though this was the great prophetical period of Israel, the message of the prophets was unheeded. The reformations that took place under such kings as Hezekiah and Josiah were superficial. The people soon returned to their sins and continued therein until "there was no remedy" (2 Chron. 36:15, 16).

Author. The human author is unknown. It is believed that Jeremiah compiled the records made by Nathan, Gad, and others.

Scope. From the reign of Jehoram over Judah and Ahaziah over Israel, to the captivity, covering a period of 308 years from 896–588 BC.

CONTENTS

As the student reads through the chapters, let him make a list of the kings of Judah and Israel, as he did in the first book. We add a parallel list of those kings:

Kings of Judah	Prophets of Judah	Kings of Israel	Prophets of Israel
Ahaziah		Jehoram	Elisha
Athaliah (queen)		Jehu	
Joash			Jonah
Amaziah		Jehoahaz	
Azariah (Uzziah)	Isaiah	Joash	
	Amos	Jeroboam II	
	Hosea	Zechariah	Joel
		Shallum	
		Menahem	
		Pekahiah	
Jotham		Pekah	
Ahaz	Micah	Hoshea	
Hezekiah	Nahum		
Manasseh			
Amon			
Josiah	Zephaniah		
	Jeremiah		
Jehoahaz			
Jehoiakim	Habakkuk		
Jehoiachin			
Zedekiah			

I. The Close of Elijah's Ministry (Chaps. 1–2:13)

1. Elijah and Ahaziah (1:1–18)
2. Translation of Elijah (2:1–13)

Who fell sick at this time? What kind of man was he? What was his great sin (Ex. 20:3; Deut. 5:7)? What judgment was pronounced upon him? How is Elijah described (1:8)?

Any appearance of cruelty that there is in the fate of the two captains and their men will be removed, on full consideration of the circumstances. God being king of Israel, Ahaziah was bound to govern the kingdom according to divine law; to apprehend the Lord's prophet for discharging a commanded duty was the act of an impious and notorious rebel. The captains abetted the king in his rebellion; and they exceeded their military duty by contemptuous insults. In using the term 'man of God,' they either spoke derisively, believing him to be no true prophet; or if they regarded him as a true prophet, the summons to him to surrender himself bound to the king was a still more flagrant insult, the language of the second captain being worse than that of the first. The punishment was inflicted, not to avenge a personal insult of Elijah, but an insult upon God in the person of His prophet; and the punishment was inflicted not by the prophet, but by the hand of God.

What had the Lord purposed (2:1)? Who was acquainted with this fact (2:3)? What miracle did Elijah perform at the Jordan? What request did Elisha make? On what condition was it granted?

II. The Ministry of Elisha (Chaps. 2:14-3:21)

The following are the chief events of Elisha's ministry:

1. Elisha's first miracle—the parting of Jordan's waters (2:14)
2. The healing of the bitter waters (2:19–22)
3. The cursing of the irreverent children (2:23–25)
4. His rebuke of the alliance of Jehoshaphat and Jehoram (3:10–27)
5. The increasing of the widow's oil (4:1–7)
6. The raising of the Shunammite woman's son (4:8–37)

    7. The healing of the deadly pottage (4:38–41)

    8. The feeding of the 100 men (4:42–44)

    9. The healing of Naaman (5:1–27)

  10. The recovery of the lost ax (6:1–7)

  11. Elisha and the Syrian host (6:8–23)

  12. Elisha's promise of food (7:1–20)

  13. His prediction of seven years of famine (8:1, 2)

  14. Elisha's visit to Ben-hadad (8:7–15)

  15. His sending of a prophet to anoint Jehu as king (9:1–10)

  16. Illness and death of Elisha (13:14–21)

Note reference to the "sons of the prophets" (2:3). We learn here that there were schools in those days where young Israelites were trained for the prophetical ministry (Compare 1 Sam. 10:5–10; 2 Kings 6:1).

Chapter 2:23 has presented difficulties to many. We quote from different commentators:

> The children mentioned here were the infidel or idolatrous young men of the place, who, affecting to disbelieve the report of his master's translation, sarcastically urged him to follow in his glorious career. The expression "bald-head" was an epithet of contempt in the East, applied even to a person with a bushy head of hair.

> The persons in question were not wanton little children, but youths who knew what they were saying and doing. Neither must we overlook the fact that these youths belonged to a city which was the center and principal seat of apostasy, and which, on this account is called "Beth Aven," i.e., the House of the Idol, instead of Bethel (house of God). They were, therefore, literally, the offspring of apostasy and they represented in general the offspring of apostates which was growing up. The older expositors suppose that the older people had incited the younger ones and that the object was to make the new head of the class of

prophets ridiculous and contemptible from the commencement of his career. When, therefore, Elisha threatened with divine punishment the impudent youths, who despised in the holy prophet the holy office to which Jehovah had called him, it was no immorality, nor was it unworthy of him; on the contrary, he did what belonged to his prophetical office. He did not, however, execute the punishment himself; he left that to Him who says, "Vengeance is mine; I will repay." It was the judgment of God that befell these youths, and indirectly, the whole city out of which they came, and it referred back to the threat of the law: "If ye walk contrary to me and will not hearken unto me . . . I will also send wild beasts among you which shall rob you of your children and destroy your cattle; and your highways shall be desolate" (Lev. 26:21, 22).

III. The Decline and Fall of Israel (Chaps. 13:22–17:41)

What nations were sent against Israel (13:22; 15:19, 29)? What were Jehovah's feelings toward Israel (13:23; 14:26, 27)? Under whose reign did Israel's captivity take place (Chap. 17)? How did he hasten Israel's judgment (17:4)? Notice God's indictment of Israel in Chaps. 17:7–23.

The forced emigration of the tribes to Assyria was a result of the despotic principle which was accepted throughout the entire Orient, that it was right to make any revolt of subjugated nations impossible. In this case it was not merely a transportation into another country, but also the commencement of the dissolution of the ten tribes as a nationality. No one particular province in Assyria was assigned to them as their dwelling-place, but several, which were far separated from one another, so that, although this or that tribe may have been kept more or less together, yet the different tribes were scattered up and down in a foreign nation, without the least organic connection with one another. They never again came together; on the contrary they were gradually lost among the surrounding nations, so that no one knows to this day, what became of them, and every attempt to discover the remains of them has been vain. In this particular the exile of the ten tribes differs from that of Judah and Benjamin. The exile in Babylon was temporary. It lasted for a definite period which had been foretold by the prophets (2 Chron. 36:21; Jer. 29:10). It was not like the Assyrian exile, a period of national dissolution. Judah did not perish in exile; it rather gained strength, and finally came back into the land of promise, whereas, of the ten tribes only a few who had joined themselves to Judah, and become a part of it, ever found their way back. The ten tribes had, by their violent separation from the rest of the nation, broken the unity of the chosen people, and, in order to maintain this separation, they had revolted from the national covenant with Jehovah. The breach of the covenant was the cornerstone of their existence as a separate nationality. Thereby also they had given up the destiny of the people of God in the world's history. They were the larger fragment of the entire nation, but they were only a separated member which was torn away from the common stock, a branch separated from the trunk, which could only wither away. After 250 years of separate existence, when all the proofs of the divine grace and faithfulness had proved vain, it was the natural fate of the ten tribes to perish and to cease to be an independent nation. The Lord removed them out of His sight; there was none left but the tribe of Judah alone (17:18). The case was different with Judah. Although it had sinned often and deeply against its God, yet it never revolted formally and in principle from the covenant, much less was its existence built upon a breach of the covenant. It remained the supporter and the preserver of the Law, and therefore also of the promise. Its deportation was indeed a heavy punishment and a well-deserved chastisement, but it did not perish thereby, nor disappear as a nation from history, but it was preserved until He

came of whom it was said: "The Lord God shall
give unto Him the throne of His father David, and
He shall reign over the house of Jacob forever; and
of His kingdom there shall be no end" (Luke 1:32,
33). —Bahr.

To take the place of the Israelites, the king of
Assyria sent colonists from his dominions. Their
idolatry brought upon them the judgment of God
in the form of the appearing of lions among them.
The king of Assyria then sent an Israelitish priest to
instruct the colonists in the religion of Jehovah. This
religion they accepted, but they still continued to
worship idols. They mingled with the remnant of the
ten tribes left in the land and from their union sprang
the Samaritans. They later abandoned idolatry and
became zealous adherents to the Law of Moses.
After the captivity, anxious to become Israelites,
they attempted to join themselves to the two tribes,
but were repelled by Ezra and Nehemiah (Ezra
4:1–3). This gave birth to hatred. The Samaritans
later built a rival temple on Mount Gerizim and
claimed that it was the true place of worship (John
4:20). This temple was later destroyed by a Jewish
king. The Jews hated them and contemptuously
referred to them as "Converts of the Lions," from
the circumstances of their conversion.

Who, in your opinion, was the best king of
Israel? The worst?

IV. The Decline and Fall of Judah (Chaps. 18-25)

The kingdom of Judah lasted about 150 years
longer than that of Israel. Their history is much
brighter than that of the latter. While Israel suffered
many changes of dynasty, the kingly line of David
was kept intact in Judah. While the history of Israel
presents a succession of revolts and usurpations,
the history of Judah is comparatively peaceful. The
preservation of Judah may be explained from the

fact that through them, the Messiah was to come.

Chapters 24, 25 record Judah's captivity. There are three stages to it:

1. Nebuchadnezzar's first invasion (24:1–2)
2. The first deportation to Babylon (24:11–16)
3. The siege and destruction of Jerusalem and the final deportation (Chap. 25)

Note that as in the case of the ten tribes, it was the rebellion of the king of Judah against the invading nation that was the cause of the final captivity (24:20). Read God's indictment of Judah (2 Chron. 36:15, 17).

Whose, in your opinion, was the golden reign of Judah? Whose was the worst reign?

CHAPTER XI

FIRST AND SECOND CHRONICLES

Introduction

Since the books of the Chronicles embrace, for the most part, the matter found in 2 Samuel and 1 and 2 Kings, we think it necessary to give only an introduction to the former.

Theme. The Greek translators of the Bible referred to these books as "The Things Omitted," because they supply much information that is not found in the books of the Kings. Though "Kings" and "Chronicles" show great similarity in the matter of their contents, they are written from different viewpoints, the former being written from the human viewpoint, the latter, from the Divine. To illustrate: 1 Kings 14:20 recording the death of Jeroboam, tells us that he "slept with his fathers." That is the human viewpoint. Second Chronicles 13:20, recording the same event, tells us that "the Lord struck him and he died." That is the divine viewpoint. One writer gives the following interesting table to show the difference between "Kings" and "Chronicles":

1. "Kings" was written shortly after the beginning of the captivity in Babylon; "Chronicles" was written shortly after the return from the captivity.
2. "Kings" was compiled by a prophet— Jeremiah; "Chronicles" by a priest—Ezra.

3. "Kings" emphasizes the throne of earthly kings; "Chronicles," the earthly throne (the temple) of the heavenly King.
4. "Kings" deals with Judah and Israel; "Chronicles," with Judah, Israel being mentioned but incidentally.
5. "Kings" is political and kingly; "Chronicles," ecclesiastical and priestly.

Author.

The writer of Chronicles is not certainly known, but probably the prevailing belief of the Jews as stated in the Talmud is correct. Ezra is declared therein to be the editor of the records written and preserved by trustworthy men. These records written by such men as Samuel, Nathan, Gad, Iddo, etc., were inspired of God and Ezra was further inspired to select from them and bring together his selections in one continuous narrative. There can be little doubt that the story in Chronicles was written by Ezra at the return from the Babylonian captivity in order to encourage the people to build the temple.

Scope. From the death of Saul to the decree of Cyrus, covering a period of 520 years from 1056 to 536 BC.

Note: It is recommended that both 1 and 2 Chronicles be read in their entirety.

EZRA

Introduction

Since the books of Ezra, Nehemiah and Esther are closely connected and deal with the same period, we give here the principal events covered by those books, in order that the student may see at a glance the history of the period following the captivity.

1. The exiles return under Zerubbabel. 536 BC
2. The rebuilding of the temple. 535 BC

3. The ministry of the prophets Haggai and Zechariah. 520 BC
4. The dedication of the temple. 515 BC
5. The events related in the book of Esther 478–473 BC
6. Ezra visits Jerusalem. 458 BC
7. Nehemiah sent to Jerusalem as governor. He rebuilds the wall. 446 BC
8. Malachi prophesies. c. 435 BC

Theme. The keynote of Ezra is restoration. A comparison with Kings and Chronicles will bear this out. Kings and Chronicles record Israel's destruction of the temple; the latter, its rebuilding. The one gives a dark picture of a nation corrupt with idolatry; the other shows us a nation completely cleansed from idol worship. The one records the neglect of the Law; the other, its restoration to its rightful place in the hearts of the people. The one records the mingling of Israel with the heathen; the other, the complete separation of Israel from heathen influence and custom. Ezra conveys a wonderful lesson of God's faithfulness. True to His promise (Jer. 29:10–14), He lifts His hand to restore His people to their land, and in so doing, He uses heathen kings—**Cyrus, Darius, Artaxerxes—as His instruments.**

Author. The fact that the book is written in the first person by Ezra (Chaps. 7 and 9) indicates that he was the author. Ezra was the first of that class known as the scribes, who were the official copyists and interpreters of the Scriptures. We read that Ezra gave himself to the study of God's Word with a view to expounding it to the people (7:10). To him has been attributed the work of settling the canon of the Old Testament; i.e., of gathering together into one book those writings that were inspired.

Scope. From the return from Babylon to the establishment in Palestine, covering a period of 79 years from about 536–457 BC.

CONTENTS

I. The Return under Zerubbabel (Chaps. 1-6)

1. Cyrus' decree (Chap. 1)
2. The returning remnant (Chap. 2)
3. The foundation of the temple laid and ancient worship restored (Chap. 3)
4. The opposition of the Samaritans (Chaps. 4, 5)
5. The dedication of the temple (Chap. 6)

Cyrus was the Persian king who overthrew the Babylonian empire, in fulfillment of divine prophecy (Isa. 14:22; Jer. 27:7; Dan. 5:28). His decree permitting the Jews' return had been foretold by Isaiah, who called Cyrus by name 200 years before the birth of the latter, referring to him as the deliverer of God's people and the rebuilder of the temple (Isa. 44:28; 45:1–4). Josephus, the Jewish historian, tells us that Daniel showed Cyrus these prophecies, and the monarch was so affected by them and so well disposed to the captive people that he issued a decree permitting them to return to their country.

Whom did God use to effect the return of His people (1:1)? Whose command did Cyrus say he was obeying (1:2)? Where did he find this command (Isa. 44:28)? Which tribes returned (1:5)? Who was their leader (1:8)? By what other name is he known (2:2 Zerubbabel)? How many returned at this time (2:64)? What was the first thing the remnant did (3:1–3)? How soon after their return was the building of the temple commenced (3:8)? What effect did this have on the people (3:10–13)? Who desired to help in the building of the temple (4:2; compare 2 Kings 17:24–41)? Did the Governor accept the help of these half-heathen people? What did this refusal lead to

(4:4)? How long did the enmity thus incurred last
(John 4:9)? What active form did their opposition
take at this time? What was the result of this
opposition? Which two prophets encouraged the
people to continue the building of the temple (5:1)?
What made it sure that the temple would be finished
(5:5)? What did the enemies of the Jews then do (5:7–
17)? What was the result of this opposition (6:1–14)?
How was the dedication of the temple celebrated
(6:17)? How many of the tribes were represented at
this time (6:17)?

II. **The Return under Ezra** (Chaps. 7-10)

1. Ezra's commission (7:1–28)
2. Ezra's companions in the return (Chap. 8)
3. Sin confessed (Chap. 9)
4. Sin forsaken (Chap. 10)

In whose reign did Ezra return to Jerusalem?
From whom was Ezra descended (7:5)? How is he
described (7:6, 12)? What was his purpose in going
to Jerusalem (7:10)? What commission was he given
(7:25, 26)? With what did Ezra begin his return
(8:21)? How did he show his absolute faith in God
(8:22)? What law concerning their relations with
heathen people had the Jews broken (9:1. Compare
Ex. 34:15, 16; Deut. 7:3)? What did the violation of
that Law always lead to (1 Kings 11:4)? What effect
did this violation of that law have on Ezra? What
were the feelings of the people upon realizing their
sin (10:1)? What covenant did they make with God?
What proclamation did Ezra make (10:7)? How great
was the conviction of the people?

Note that the action of the Jews in putting away
their heathen wives and children was rather a strin-
gent one, but it should be remembered that in the
past, intermarriage with the heathen had led to sin
and idolatry, and it was necessary that the tribe of

Judah should remain pure for through them was to come the Messiah.

NEHEMIAH

Theme. This book centers around a person—Nehemiah. It is an autobiography of a man who sacrificed a life of ease and luxury in order to help his needy brethren in Jerusalem. It describes a man who combined spirituality with practicality—one who knew how both to pray and work. Absolutely fearless, he refused to compromise with enemies on the outside or with sin on the inside. After rebuilding the wall of Jerusalem and effecting many sweeping reforms among the people, he humbly gave God the glory for all that had been accomplished. The main lesson taught by his life is that prayer and perseverance will overcome all obstacles.

Author. Nehemiah

Scope. From Nehemiah's journey to Jerusalem to the restoration of temple worship, covering a period of about 12 years from 446–434 BC.

CONTENTS

I. The Building of the Wall of Jerusalem
(Chaps. 1-6)

  1. Nehemiah's prayer and commission (Chaps. 1, 2)

  2. The builders of the wall (Chap. 3)

  3. The opposition of the Samaritans (Chap. 4)

4. The nobles rebuked for their oppression of the people (Chap. 5)
5. The completion of the work of building (Chap. 6)

What news did Nehemiah receive (1:2, 3)? What effect did it have on him? How often did he pray for Israel (1:6)? What position did Nehemiah hold?

> The cupbearer, in ancient Oriental courts was always a person of rank and importance; and, from the confidential nature of his duties, and his frequent access to the royal presence, possessed of great influence. Xenophon, a Greek historian, has particularly remarked the polished and graceful manners in which the cup-bearers of the Median and Persian monarchs performed their duty of presenting the wine to their royal master. Having washed the cup in the king's presence, and poured into their left hand a little of the wine which they drank off in his presence, then they handed the cup to him, not grasped, but lightly held with the tips of their thumb and fingers.

What led indirectly to Nehemiah's being sent to Jerusalem (2:1, 2)? Note that Nehemiah's fear is explained by the fact that it was considered highly unbecoming to appear in the presence of the king with any signs of sorrow or mourning. What did Nehemiah do before making his request to the king (2:4)? Who were grieved at his coming to Jerusalem (2:10, 19)? What was the first attempt to discourage Nehemiah (4:1–3)? How did he treat this attempt (vv. 4–6)? What second attempt was made to discourage him (4:7, 8)? To what did he then resort (v. 9)? What other discouragement came at this time (4:10, 16)? What precautions did Nehemiah take against a surprise attack (4:16–23)? What had the people been compelled to do on account of their poverty (5:1–3)? Who had been guilty of oppression

(v. 7)? What example had Nehemiah set before the nobles (5:14–19)? What other attempts were made to hinder Nehemiah's work (Chap. 6)? What does 6:11 reveal concerning Nehemiah's character? What fact discouraged his enemies (6:16)? How long did it take to build the wall (6:15)?

II. Revival of Religion and Re-establishment of Worship (Chaps. 7–13:3)

1. Register of the people (Chap. 7)
2. The reading of the law (Chap. 8)
3. The repentance and reconsecration of the people (Chaps. 9, 10)
4. Resettlement at Jerusalem (Chap. 11)
5. Dedication of the wall and restoration of temple service (Chaps. 12 to 13:3)

Whom did Nehemiah leave in charge of Jerusalem while he returned to the king of Persia (7:2)? What precautions were the people to take against surprise attacks (7:3)?

Before leaving, Nehemiah took another register of the people based upon the one made by Ezra. This was for the purpose of distributing the land according to the ancestral abode of each family, and for ascertaining with accuracy to whom the duty legally belonged of ministering before the altar and conducting the various services of the temple. Nehemiah 7:73 tells the result of this registration; namely that all the families were in their own cities.

Who later joined Nehemiah (8:1)? For what purpose? What was the command of Moses concerning the public reading of the Law (Deut. 31:9–13)? How many of the people gathered to listen to the reading of the Law (8:2)? Who explained its meaning (8:7, 8)? What effect did it have on the people (8:9)? What other effect did it produce (8:12)? How many days did this reading continue (8:18)?

What followed the reading of the Law (9:1–3)? What historical events were reviewed in the prayer of the Levites? What was then done (9:38)? How many signed this covenant? What did they covenant to do (10:28–39)?

Chapter 11 records the settlement of the people at Jerusalem. Since that city was the metropolis of the land, it was necessary that the seat of government and an adequate population should be there for its defense and for the custody of its buildings. Accordingly every tenth man of Judah and Benjamin was chosen by lot to become a permanent inhabitant of that city.

III. Correction of Abuses (Chaps. 13:4-31)

1. Violation of temple's sanctity. (vv. 4 to 9)
2. Violation of law concerning Levites (vv. 10–14)
3. Violation of the sabbath rest (vv. 15–22)
4. The violation of the law of separation (vv. 23–31)

After his first reforms, Nehemiah returned to the court of the king of Persia (13:6). On his return, he found that the priesthood and people had lapsed into their old sins. The high priest was entertaining a heathen governor within the sacred precincts of the temple; the support of the priesthood had been neglected; the spirit of commercialism was threatening the sanctity of the Sabbath day; and many of the people had contracted unlawful unions with the heathen. With his characteristic zeal and energy. Nehemiah quickly corrected their abuses.

CHAPTER XII

ESTHER

Theme. The book of Esther has a peculiarity that distinguishes it from any other book in the Bible: namely, the name of God is not once mentioned, neither are there any references to the Jewish Law or religion. But if God's name is not mentioned, there are abundant evidences of His working and of His care for His people. The book records God's deliverance of His people from a threatened destruction. As truly as He saved His people from Pharaoh's power, He delivered Israel from the hands of the wicked Haman. In the former case, the deliverance was effected by a manifestation of His power and a revelation of Himself; but in the latter case, He remained unseen to His people and enemies, effecting salvation through human channels, and by natural means.

> The very absence of the name of God is its chief beauty and should not be considered as a blot upon it. Matthew Henry says, "If the name of God is not here, His finger is." This book is, as Dr. Pierson called it, "The Romance of Providence." By Providence we mean that in all the affairs and events of human life, individual and national, God has a part and share. But that control is a secret and hidden one. Hence in this wonderful story which teaches the reality of the Divine providence, the name of God does not appear, only as the eye of faith sees the Divine factor in human history; but to the attentive observer all history is a Burning Bush aflame with the mysterious presence. Jewish tradition gives Deuteronomy 31:18 as another reason why God's name is not mentioned. Because

of their sin, God had hidden His face from Israel. Yet, though hiding His face, He was not forgetful or unconcerned about His people, though He did it under a veil. —Lee.

The message of the book may be summed up as follows: The Reality of Divine Providence.

Author. Unknown. Possibly Mordecai (See 9:20). Some believe Ezra wrote it.

Scope. Between the 6th and 7th chapters of Ezra, before Ezra left for Jerusalem.

CONTENTS

Following the suggestion of Robert Lee of the Mildmay Bible School, we center the contents of the book around the three feasts mentioned therein.

   I. The Feast of Ahasuerus (Chap. 1, 2)
  II. The Feast of Esther (Chap. 3–7)
III. The Feast of Purim (Chap. 8–10)

I. The Feast of Ahasuerus (Chaps. 1, 2)

  1. Vashti's disobedience (Chap. 1)
  2. Esther's coronation (2:1–20)
  3. Mordecai saves the king's life (2:21–23)

The refusal of Vashti to obey an order that required her to make an indecent exposure of herself before a company of drunken revellers, was becoming with the modesty of her sex and her rank as queen, for according to Persian customs, the queen, even more than the wives of other men, was excluded from the public gaze; and had not the king's blood been heated with wine, or his reason overpowered by the force of offended pride, he would have perceived that his own honor, as well as hers, was consulted by her dignified conduct. The wise men whom the king consulted were probably the magi, without whose advice as to the proper time of doing a thing the Persian kings never did take any step whatever; and the persons named were the 'seven counsellors' who formed the state ministry. The combined wisdom of all, it seems, was enlisted to consult with the king what course should be taken after so unprecedented an occurrence as Vashti's disobedience to the royal summons. It is scarcely possible for us to imagine the astonishment produced by such a refusal in a country where the will of the sovereign was absolute. The assembled grandees were petrified with horror at the daring affront; alarm for the consequences that might ensue to each of them in his own household next seized on their minds, and the sounds of bacchanalian revelry were hushed into deep and anxious consultation as to what punishment to inflict on the refractory queen. —Jamieson, Fausset and Brown.

Notice what is said in verse 19 concerning the laws of the Medes and Persians. The Persians seem to have affected such a degree of wisdom in the construction of their laws, that they never could be amended or repealed; and this formed the ground of the saying "The laws of the Medes and Persians that change not." Ahasuerus was probably sorry for his treatment of Vashti (2:1), but according to the law which made the word of a Persian king irrevocable, she could not be recalled by law.

Chapter 2:3, 4 refers to a harsh custom of the East. When the order came forth from the royal court for a girl to present herself before the king, however unwilling the parents were, they dared not refuse. Thus Esther was compelled to enter the court of Ahasuerus. It should be noted that, in the East, where polygamy prevailed, it was considered no disgrace for a girl to belong to the "harem" of a ruler. Every one there was considered a wife of the king.

Notice that Mordecai had instructed Esther to conceal her nationality (2:10). If Esther had made this known, it would have interferred with her advancement to the rank of queen, as the Jews were generally despised. In this injunction of Mordecai to

Esther, we see an indication of Divine leading, for was it not by her being queen that Esther was able to save her people?

Chapter 2:21 mentions another link in the chain of God's providence. Mordecai protects the life of the king against plotters, and this is recorded in the chronicles of the kingdom. This incident played an important part in the deliverance of the Jews, as we shall see later.

II. **The Feast of Esther** (Chaps. 3-7)

    1. Haman's plot (Chap. 3)
    2. The Jews' mourning (Chap. 4)
    3. Esther's petition (Chap. 5)
    4. Mordecai's exaltation (Chap. 6)
    5. Haman's death (Chap. 7)

The quotations given in the following section are taken from Jamieson, Fausset and Brown's commentary.

> The obsequious homage of prostration, not entirely foreign to the manners of the East, had not been claimed by former viziers; but Haman required that all subordinate officers of the court should bow before him with their faces to the earth. But to Mordecai it seemed that such an attitude of profound reverence was due only to God. Haman, being an Amalekite, one of a doomed and accursed race, was doubtless another element in the refusal; and on hearing that the offender was a Jew, whose non-conformity was grounded on religious scruples, the magnitude of the affront appeared so much the greater, as the example of Mordecai would be imitated by his countrymen. Had the homage been a simple token of civil respect, Mordecai would not have refused it; but the Persian kings demanded a sort of adoration which even the Greeks reckoned it degradation to express, and which, to Mordecai would have been a violation of the second commandment.

Haman was so incensed at Mordecai's refusal to worship him that he resolved to destroy the whole Jewish race, and in order to appoint a day for the execution of his purpose, he cast Pur; i.e., he cast lots.

> In resorting to this method of ascertaining the most auspicious day for putting his atrocious scheme into execution, Haman acted as the kings and nobles of Persia have always done, never engaging in any enterprise without consulting the astrologers and being satisfied as to the lucky hour. Vowing revenge, but scorning to lay hands on a single victim, he meditated the extirpation of the whole Jewish race, who, he knew, were sworn enemies of his countrymen, and by artfully representing them as a people who were aliens in manners and customs and habits, and enemies to the rest of his subjects, procured the king's sanction of the intended massacre. One motive used in urging his point was addressed to the king's love of money. Fearing lest his master should object that the extermination of a numerous body of his subjects would seriously depress the public revenue, Haman promised to make up the loss (3:9).

Though, as we said in our introduction, there were no direct references to Jewish religion, the fact of Esther's and Mordecai's fasting implies prayer to God. Notice also that though the name of God is not mentioned, chapter 4:14 clearly teaches faith in God's care and protection. Mordecai seems to have a full assurance that God will deliver His people and that in God's providence, Esther had come to the throne for the purpose of delivering her people.

Did natural circumstances seem to promise Esther a hearing from the king (4:11)? What did Esther expect (4:16)? How was God's influence manifested in her behalf (5:3)? Did she immediately plead for her people's deliverance? What was to happen before she did this (6:1, 10)? What Scripture does 7:10 illustrate (Prov. 26:27; Psa. 9:15)?

III. The Feast of Purim (Chaps. 8:1–10:3)

1. The king's decree allowing the Jews to protect themselves (Chap. 8)
2. The vengeance of the Jews (9:1–19)
3. The institution of the feast of Purim (9:20–32)
4. Mordecai's greatness (10:1–3)

Since the laws of the Medes and Persians were irrevocable (1:19; Dan. 6:8), the king's command to destroy the Jews could not be reversed. But in order to counteract this order, the king gave permission to the Jews to defend themselves. With the support of the king and government, and of a Jewish prime minister, victory was assured. But behind all these natural means, it was the unseen God who was protecting His own.

What were the feelings of the Jews on hearing of the king's decree (8:16, 17)? What effect did it produce on the heathen (8:17)? How many of their enemies did the Jews slay (9:16)? How did the Jews celebrate their victory?

"They called these days Purim, after the name of Pur [lots]" (9:26).

Pur, in the Persian language, signifies lot; and the feast of Purim, or lots, has reference to the time having been pitched upon by Haman through the decision of the lot (3:7). In consequence of the signal national deliverance which divine providence gave them from the infamous machinations of Haman, Mordecai ordered the Jews to commemorate the event by an anniversary festival which was to last two days in accordance with the two days' war of defense they had to maintain. There was a slight difference in the time of this festival; for the Jews in the provinces, having defended themselves against their enemies on the thirteenth, devoted the fourteenth to festivity; whereas their brethren in Shushan, having extended the work over two days, did not observe their thanksgiving feast till the fifteenth. But this was remedied by the authority which fixed the fourteenth and fifteenth of the month of Adar. It became a season of sunny memories to the universal body of Jews; and by the letters of Mordecai, scattered through all parts of the Persian empire, it was established as an annual feast, the celebration of which is still kept up. On both days of the feast, the modern Jews read the book of Esther in their synagogues. The copy must not be printed, but written on vellum in the form of a roll; and the names of the ten sons of Haman are written on it in a peculiar manner, being ranged, they say, like so many bodies on a gibbet. The reader must pronounce all the names in one breath. Whenever Haman's name is pronounced, they make a terrible noise in the synagogues. Some drum with their feet on the floor and the boys have mallets with which they knock and make a noise. They prepare themselves for their carnival by a previous fast, which should continue three days, in imitation of Esther's but they have mostly reduced it to one day.

Lessons from the Book of Esther

1. Though sometimes the good may suffer and the evil prosper, God will eventually reverse the order. Haman, a cruel tyrant planned the destruction of Mordecai and his nation. In the end, Haman was degraded and Mordecai exalted.

2. God's care for His people may not always be an apparent fact, but nevertheless, it is being exercised. The name of God is not mentioned in this book, but evidences of His care and protection abound. One writer illustrates this truth by the figure of a stage manager, who, though hidden behind the scenes, plays an important part in the staging of a play.

> Careless seems the great Avenger; History's
>   pages but record
> One death-grapple in the darkness 'twixt old
>   systems and the word;

Truth forever on the scaffold, Wrong forever
   on the throne—
Yet that scaffold sways the future and, behind
   the dim unknown,
Standeth God within the shadow, keeping
   watch above His own.

—Lowell

3. God foresees and provides for every emergency; with Him, nothing happens by chance. God foresaw from the beginning the intended destruction of His people, and He provided for that emergency. A poor Jewish girl becomes queen and is thus able to save her people. God foresaw that Haman would attempt to destroy Mordecai; accordingly He so arranges events that a spell of sleeplessness on the part of the king leads to Mordecai's exaltation. God foresaw that since the decrees of the Medes and Persians were unchangeable, the Jews would have to fight for their lives; so He puts fear upon the people and gives the Jews favor in the sight of the governors.

4. God's providence takes in details. The accident of the king's sleeplessness, his fancy to have the records read, the reader's stumbling accidentally on the account of Mordecai's act in saving the king's life, the king's happening to receive Esther when she came unbidden—all these seemingly accidental and insignificant events were used by God to deliver His people.

NOTES

NOTES